CULTIVATING CIVILITY

CULTIVATING CIVILITY

Practical Ways to Improve a Dysfunctional Library

Jo Henry, Joe Eshleman, and Richard Moniz

ALA Editions

CHICAGO | 2020

Extensive effort has gone into ensuring the reliability of the information in this book; however, the publisher makes no warranty, express or implied, with respect to the material contained herein.

ISBNs
978-0-8389-4716-6 (paper)
978-0-8389-4724-1 (PDF)
978-0-8389-4723-4 (ePub)
978-0-8389-4725-8 (Kindle)

Library of Congress Control Number: 2019954457

Cover design by Alejandra Diaz; image © retrostar, Adobe Stock.

Text design in the Calisto MT and Helvetica typefaces.

♾ This paper meets the requirements of ANSI/NISO Z39.48-1992 (Permanence of Paper).

Printed in the United States of America

22 21 22 21 20   5 4 3 2 1

*Dedicated to all who are dealing
with challenges in the library workplace
and looking for solutions.*

CONTENTS

Part IV   The Functional Organization

ACKNOWLEDGMENTS

We would like to thank the ALA Editions | ALA Neal Schuman editorial board for their overwhelming support of our book. We especially want to say a huge "thank you" to our editor Jamie Santoro for all her guidance and assistance with this project. As with our other books, she has provided invaluable feedback and counsel throughout the process. We would also like to thank all of the other members of the ALA Editions | ALA Neal Schuman team who work behind the scenes with great success. Thank you also to Rob Christopher, marketing coordinator, and his staff. Additionally, we would like to recognize Angela Gwizdala, director of editorial, design, and production, and her editorial staff for seeing us through the final stages of the book.

As in all our writing projects, the support of spouses, family, and friends is invaluable. They too sacrifice as we take time away from them for research and writing. Without their continuous support, our work would not be possible.

INTRODUCTION

When we wrote our original work, *The Dysfunctional Library: Challenges and Solutions to Workplace Relationships* (2018), we also completed a survey of over 4,100 library staff which indicated that incivility and dysfunction were prevalent in the field. Our hope was to shine some light on this topic and provide some ideas for solutions to those in need. After the book's release, we were contacted to do workshops on the topic both in-person and online. These additional interactions with library staff and administrators also confirmed the pervasiveness of these workplace issues. Inevitably, at the end of our workshops attendees would ask the same questions: "What do we do now? Can you provide more solutions? What's next?"

Writing a follow-up book was never in our plans, but we felt compelled to come together one more time in an attempt to answer these questions. While the first book provided some solutions, it was primarily focused on defining the different kinds and causes of library workplace dysfunction. This new book, *Cultivating Civility: Practical Ways to Improve a Dysfunctional Library* is just that—a book of solutions. We cannot possibly provide a solution to every problem that exists in the library workplace, but we can provide additional information and stimulate thought and discussion towards that goal. Additionally, we wanted the book to be for everyone. As a result, we divided this book into four parts—individual, team, leader, and organization—focusing solutions in each part on those respective viewpoints.

Chapters 1–5 deal with the functional self, and the discussion begins in chapter 1 with gaining an increased understanding and awareness of oneself. We have always felt that self-reflection and self-awareness are key starting points when we explore issues affecting us in the workplace. Chapters 2 and 3 provide tips for interpersonal communication, conversations, and assertiveness and then offer a deeper view of communication. Communication issues seem to be a prominent concern in many organizations, and libraries are no different in this respect. Individuals who are focused on handling interpersonal conflict in challenging or even toxic workplace situations will benefit from chapter 4. Chapter 5 concludes the book's first part on individuals by focusing on wellness and self-care. Unless we make sure that we are as mentally and physically healthy as we can be, we will not be able to address the concerns and stressors in the workplace very effectively. This chapter provides some common approaches to improving one's lifestyle in this regard.

Chapters 6, 7, and 8 all deal with teamwork and shed light on how to form and sustain good library teams. Organizing a functional team is the focus of chapter 6, which lays out how to best use teams within your library and provides solutions for misaligned teams and dissenters. Additionally, making a concerted effort to create diverse work groups and how to develop a good team mindset are also explored. Turning to chapter 7, how teams can communicate to prevent information silos and span boundaries is explored. In chapter 8, the overarching solution of using a number of different communication methods to improve teams is offered. An often overlooked aspect of communication—that is, the preferred methods that library staff have—is also deliberated upon in this chapter. As is the case throughout the book, the chapters in this part provide real-life examples from libraries that help to solve dysfunction hurdles.

Solutions for functional leaders are provided in chapters 9–14. While self-awareness is addressed earlier in the book from a general perspective, chapter 9 focuses exclusively on this topic as it applies to leaders. Often the self-awareness of the leaders can have a dramatic impact on the culture of the library as a whole. The value of authenticity, conveying vision, role-modeling, and empathy as displayed by leaders is explored in chapter 10. These qualities in leaders can have a very positive impact on the library workplace. In chapter 11, leader communication is the primary topic. Treating staff equally, developing a positive workplace, encouraging staff to thrive, and showing inclusivity are all goals of the highly communicative library leader. If the leader can work toward these goals when communicating, an environment of trust is established and dysfunction is greatly diminished. Chapter 12 focuses on conflict management as practiced by leaders, who are often tasked with this as a major function of their role. Chapter 13 points out that allowing library staff to work on projects of interest, providing them with adequate time and balanced workloads, and taking time for team-bonding can work well in the library. The leader who facilitates collaboration in these ways and also takes time to create diversity among her staff will be greatly rewarded. In chapter 14, how to manage staff members' resistance to change is considered. A lament heard over and over again in dysfunctional libraries is that staff do not feel part of a unified team and they feel as though their work serves no purpose. In this chapter, library leadership is called to engage employees in a change process which may help to alleviate this morale-buster.

The final part of this book explores solutions for a functional organization. Chapter 15 explores the need to hire the right employees, which is a critical element in setting the library up for success. Chapter 16 examines how it is not just personalities, but also organizational structures that can either detract or contribute to a library's success. The importance of developing a trusting workplace environment is examined in chapter 17. Among the solutions in this regard are forming a balanced psychological contract with employees, as well as promoting opportunities for employee engagement and growth. The organization part of this book concludes with a look at various types of training that can be used to minimize dysfunction. These include training for bias, empathy, conflict management, and diversity.

While many readers will find every chapter of this book useful, the design allows for targeted reading as well. The solutions (in part I) for a more functional self may benefit all readers. Other parts provide solution perspectives depending on one's position and function in the library organization. We hope that there are benefits for everyone in this book. So let the page turn and the exploration of solutions for library dysfunction begin!

PART I

The Functional Individual

Understand Yourself First

Without self-awareness one will be doomed to failure from the start when addressing workplace problems. Self-awareness, therefore, is the crucial starting point for all of the content in this book. Without understanding ourselves and how we are perceived by others, we will be trying to solve problems in the dark, especially those that involve interpersonal relationships. Self-awareness is not only critical for library managers but for anyone working in a library setting. In the words of one scholar speaking on civility, "I now see that bad behavior reflects a lack of self-awareness. We don't want to hurt others but we do."[1] It is important to note that, while difficult, self-awareness can be improved. Put simply, increasing our self-awareness has wide-ranging benefits.

General Self-Awareness

The modern concept of self-awareness, especially as it applies to the library workplace, is the ability to know what one's own goals, values, and behaviors are and then also be able to see oneself from an outsider's or coworker's perspective. It is important to note that while self-awareness is of critical importance, possessing it alone does not mean that an individual is effective. By way of example, someone could see themselves as manipulative and controlling while others see them that way too. Thus, this individual could theoretically be self-aware and still not be a great person to work with. These people are labeled as "aware don't care," and it is often impossible to change their approach. Often, these individuals believe they are better than others, and they also genuinely believe that leading through intimidation is a logical way to lead and manage.[2] Without self-awareness a person will continually be thwarted in efforts to be the most successful version of themselves. It takes both a willingness and a desire to do good, as well as self-awareness, to be effective and functional. One's ability to accomplish tasks is itself inextricably connected to self-awareness.[3] Essentially, a belief in one's self leads to better achievement.[4]

Those who lack self-awareness, Tasha Eurich states, "won't listen to, or accept, critical feedback. They cannot empathize with, or take the perspective of, others. They have difficulty 'reading a room' and tailoring their message to their audience. They possess an inflated opinion of their contributions and performance. They are hurtful to others without realizing it. They take credit for successes and blame others for failures."[5] It is hard to imagine anyone wanting to work in a library where employees are described this way. And yet, there may be someone in the library workplace who fits this description in part or whole. Often, our behavior falls on a spectrum. On some days and in some situations, individuals may be more self-aware than in others. Also, while the very point of self-awareness on a deeper level is understanding one's underlying emotions and motivations, when one is upset, angry, or stressed it can be much more challenging to maintain a sense of self-awareness. There are ways, however, that individuals can improve their ability to handle difficult situations while maintaining self-awareness.

Self-awareness is most definitely not achieved by beating oneself up over everything said and done. According to Eurich, "frequent self-analyzers are more depressed and anxious and experience poorer well-being."[6] At some point, many of us experience stress and anxiety about how we could have done something better or differently. While we should certainly consider our past actions, it is essential that we do not go too far in dwelling on the past. This can lead to depression, anxiety, and, in the long run, an inability to change for the better. The goal is not just better performance, but a better work experience and life in general. This must be kept in the forefront as individuals confront, through self-awareness, their strengths and weaknesses.

Being too self-critical also relates to the concept of "vocational awe." Fobazi Ettarh, among others, notes that this is a significant problem in librarianship. According to Ettarh, "'vocational awe' refers to the set of ideas, values, and assumptions librarians have about themselves and the profession that result in beliefs that libraries as institutions are inherently good and sacred, and therefore beyond critique."[7] Many a librarian considers librarianship *a calling*. The use of this word has some far-reaching consequences in how library workers see themselves. This, in turn, has significant implications for any discussion of self-awareness in the library workplace. To begin with, there is much evidence to suggest that this way of thinking is similar to or connected to religion and the history of religion, or to religious faith and ideas. Librarians often think of their work as enabling a higher good. What does vocational awe mean to the individual library employee? Ettarh notes that "awe is used as a method of eliciting obedience from people in the presence of something bigger than themselves."[8] The key word here is obedience. He goes on to state: "Awe is easily weaponized against the worker, allowing anyone to deploy a vocational purity test in which the worker can be accused of not being devout or passionate enough to serve without complaint."[9] This "weaponization" can be used to justify librarians, say, not getting a lunch break or not taking a needed mental health day. How can someone think of their own interests when the work being done is so sacred? Vocational awe ties to pay and benefits as well. "Through its enforcement of awe through the promotion of dramatic and heroic narratives, the institution gains free, or reduced price, labor."[10] This is a real problem for library staff. It serves as a justification for job creep and for trying to live up to some sort of martyred status. It is good when library staff are passionate about what they do, but when work and roles are viewed through the lens of self-awareness, staff must recognize and resist the tendency to become, in essence, a doormat.

Self-Awareness Solutions

So what are some ways to improve our self-awareness? A good beginning is where the text left off above when considering the issue of being critical of oneself or suffering from "vocational awe." Jean Pincott notes the dangers of having an "inner critic." Individuals must become aware that they are in essence sometimes putting themselves down with self-reflection.

One suggestion for combating this is to, as odd as it sounds, refer to oneself in the third person. By distancing ourselves from the issue at hand we can gain a more objective perspective. Another approach Pincott shares is the practice that some therapists use in getting adults to consider when their inner critic first materialized. They are then encouraged to essentially befriend a younger version of themselves. Presumably, one would not treat another person, especially one cared about, with the same harshness as oneself, but this is also true when "talking" to one's younger self. Another pitfall noted by Pincott is that individuals can fall into a pattern of dichotomous thinking whereby past actions are either "good" or "bad" when often they are not that absolute.[11] The key idea is to find a way, without berating oneself, to learn from one's mistakes. So, one thing to understand about working to improve self-awareness is that it is *not* an excuse to attack oneself. Pincott's solution to this problem is important to have at hand when an individual feels they are doing so. If a friend made a mistake or provided a less than ideal answer in a job interview, would one say to her, "That was a stupid thing to say. You really don't interview well and don't deserve that job." No, of course not. Yet, perhaps some version of this is what many of us would potentially do . . . to ourselves. But what if this situation was thought of in the third person? How might that look? How about something like this: "You didn't answer that one question well, but now you know you need to do better next time. How could you have better responded in case you have another opportunity to do so in the future?" It is readily apparent here that when the framing changes, there is a greater opening for future success. One additional suggestion from McQueen and Klein, in their extensive analysis of research on self-affirmation, is worth considering as well. Recognizing our best qualities, especially when we are about to face criticism, can prevent us from falling down a rabbit hole of doubt and despair and instead use the opportunity for purposeful reflection.[12]

Another Key to Self-Awareness

Self-awareness includes both how we see ourselves and how others see us. Often individuals get "stuck" on one side of that equation. There needs to be a balance between a deep understanding of ourselves and a commitment to our core personal values, on the one hand, with an awareness of how others perceive us. Focusing on just one side misses the point entirely. Another key way that individuals can improve their self-awareness, therefore, is to assess where they are right now. Eurich describes the balance between how one sees oneself and how others see one as the key to being a self-aware person. Other tools will be discussed in this chapter, but a free online "Insight Quiz" associated with Tasha Eurich's book *Insight: Why We're Not as Self-Aware as We Think, and How Seeing Ourselves Clearly Helps Us Succeed at Work and in Life* (2017) is available at www.insight-book .com. Eurich is one of the leading scholars in this area. The information in her book is based on her own studies, in addition to an analysis of more than 800 other studies on the topic of self-awareness.[13] Her quiz asks the quiz-taker questions about how they see themselves, and then asks the quiz-taker to e-mail a trusted friend or colleague to fill the quiz out for them as well. The idea behind this tool is that, when looking at self-ratings and the ratings of a colleague, one should see a commonality between them. If not, it indicates that one's self-awareness may be skewed.[14] This allows the individual to better understand what her personal values are and how those are translating or not translating into action.

SOLUTIONS STORY

How Changing My Desk Location Improved My Quality of Life

CARALYN ANNE CHAMPA

When I first started as the public services librarian at the US Army Garrison Italy in 2015, I set up a desk on the main floor of the library in a central area. My goal was to be at the heart of the library in order to help *everyone*. However, in the brief moments I would get to sit down at that desk, I would respond to mainly directional or computer questions. It wasn't the patrons' fault—I had chosen to put the desk there. But I found that I was getting zero program-related work done, and I wasn't even able to respond to an e-mail without interruption. A month ago, I moved my primary workspace upstairs to a slightly more private setting—still no walls, but at least I'm not by the self-reservation computer anymore. This practical change has made a huge difference for me. I find that I am more productive and less stressed. In addition, I have challenged myself to set time aside for reflection about recent programs. This helps me capture important details and powerful moments. For example, during a recent Makerspace Petting Zoo, I observed a whole family building magnetic tile structures together. At one point, the little girl said, "I've never built anything like this before!" If I hadn't made time to sit down and reflect after the program, I could have easily overlooked this young patron's moment of joy and discovery. I also created a tracking sheet so I can better capture the reference and readers' advisory questions I field on a daily basis. Since readers' advisory is one of my favorite aspects of my work, this time spent remembering my interactions with customers is quite pleasant. It will help me with future readers' advisory questions, since I will have a record of past connections and recommendations. In addition, it is an artifact that my colleagues can search and refer to when I am not available for "live" assistance. I am actively seeking other practical changes to try out in hopes of improving my general well-being while at work, so that I can contribute to the library and our community from a more centered and joyful place.

As previously noted, Eurich points out other problems with those who lack self-awareness, such as not being able to accept feedback, not being able to see others' perspectives, and not knowing how to tailor a message. Hurting others inadvertently, as well as claiming credit for work done by others or by the team as a whole, can also stem from a lack of self-awareness. These shortcomings, however, imply some immediate ways in which we can improve our awareness. For one thing, we can *listen*. This will be reiterated many times in this book. The minute we begin to listen we are opening the door to understanding. And then there is *humility*. Individuals may be great at their job or other things in life, but it is still critically important to recognize the efforts of others. One of the most tone-deaf things we could do would be to claim sole credit for something that someone else or the team has accomplished. We should *recognize our impact on others*. We should consider how other people have different experiences and backgrounds, and thereby recognize that something we may have said or done which we thought was innocuous could actually be hurtful to someone else. Referring to an earlier point, the idea is not to berate oneself, but rather to try to understand the other person's perception of one's actions or words, apologize as appropriate, and then move on with a deeper understanding. Martel and Perkins note that a key part of successful self-awareness is owning up to one's mistakes.[15]

Yet another way to approach self-awareness is to think of oneself as having a reputation or, in marketing terms, a brand. Hubert Rampersad says that "your personal brand is the synthesis of all expectations, images, and perceptions it creates in the minds of others, when they see or hear your name."[16] Furthermore, Busch and Davis discuss personal branding as it connects to self-awareness. "We assert that true self-awareness is the foundation for creating a personal brand."[17] How does one go about understanding a personal brand? One way is through various tools intended to give individuals a more complete picture of themselves. We have already mentioned a simple quiz about self-awareness. It is important to recognize, however, that there are many tools that have added depth if you want to take this further. For example, Busch and David suggest using StrengthsFinder and 360Reach. In conjunction with publishing their book *Now, Discover Your Strengths* (2001), Buckingham and Clifton created StrengthsFinder, which, according to its website, has been used by more than 20,000,000 people.[18] The test costs $50, but it helps to determine one's natural strengths. The test has limitations, and there have been various criticisms of this tool, but it would be hard to deny that reaching an enhanced understanding of one's strengths can be useful in the quest for greater self-awareness. For the same price of $50 individuals can also gain access to 360Reach. This tool is based on the concept of 360-degree feedback. "According to Edwards and Ewen, the first published professional literature on this approach dates from 1993. The idea behind 360-degree feedback is to have not just a supervisor but others such as peers, direct subordinates and, in some cases, customers or vendors rate an employee's performance."[19] As discussed above, self-awareness consists of matching up our own perceptions of ourselves and our values with others' perceptions of us. 360-degree feedback, while not without its critics, entails having a variety of individuals answer a series of questions that relate to how one is perceived. Thus, individuals can triangulate not just a single external perception against their own, but do so from multiple points of view. How those views differ or reveal the same information can be telling. Does everyone have the same views of oneself across the groups? The next step is up to the individual, but at least they would have the information to consider.

Finally, one last word needs to be said about the concept of a "beginner's mind." Frequently used in conjunction with mindfulness, this term implies that sometimes our past experiences and existing biases impede our ability to be self-aware. But if individuals approach things with a beginner's mind and try to shed some of their predetermined ways of viewing the world or a situation, they may gain a deeper understanding. Critically, they may find a new way to view themselves and their actions.

What Is My Work Personality?

Some authors argue that our workplace self-awareness can differ from our self-awareness in other situations or roles, and the former constitutes one element of what is referred to as our "work personality." According to Barrick and Mount, one's workplace personality can be "an enduring predictor of a number of significant behaviors at work, behaviors that cannot be predicted adequately by general mental ability, job knowledge, or the situation itself."[20] Much of what has been said already can be applied here. In analyzing our workplace personality, we can ask ourselves a series of questions: "How do I behave at work? How do I react at work in a variety of different situations? How am I viewed at work by my colleagues? How might my work personality differ or not differ from how I behave in other environments?" Again, there is no simple answer to these questions, but by understanding that everyone has a work personality, we can better understand our interactions with others and seek ways to improve our experiences in the library.

Conclusion

Understanding oneself is very important if one is to be successful in the library workplace. Individuals must understand themselves and their core values. That said, they need to be careful not to become "self-absorbed" in the process. Library staff must also be able to accurately perceive how others see them. This requires the ability to receive and consider potentially critical feedback.

QUESTIONS FOR DISCUSSION

- What are the core values I bring to the workplace?
- How do I think I am perceived in my library by coworkers?
- How do my coworkers really see me?
- How can I be more receptive to feedback?
- If I get more feedback, what might I do with it to improve my success in the role I play in my library?

NOTES

1. Christine Porath, *Mastering Civility: A Manifesto for the Workplace* (New York: Grand Central, 2016).
2. Tasha Eurich, *Insight: Why We're Not as Self-Aware as We Think, and How Seeing Ourselves Clearly Helps Us Succeed at Work and in Life* (New York: Crown, 2017), 242.
3. Albert Bandura, "Self-Efficacy Mechanism in Human Agency," *American Psychologist* 37, no. 2 (February 1982): 123.
4. Linda Dudar, Shelleyann Scott, and Donald E. Scott, "The Self-Aware and Discerning Change Agent," in *Accelerating Change in Schools: Leading Rapid, Successful, and Complex Change Initiatives,* Advances in Educational Administration 27 (Bingley, UK: Emerald, 2017), 88.
5. Tasha Eurich, "Working with People Who Aren't Self-Aware," *Harvard Business Review* (October 19, 2018): 28–29.
6. Tasha Eurich, "What Self-Awareness Really Is (and How to Cultivate It)," *Harvard Business Review* (January 4, 2018): 8.
7. Fobazi Ettarh, "Vocational Awe and the Lies We Tell Ourselves," *In the Library with the Lead Pipe,* January 10, 2018, http://www.inthelibrarywiththeleadpipe.org/2018/vocational-awe/.
8. Ettarh, "Vocational Awe and the Lies We Tell Ourselves."
9. Ettarh, "Vocational Awe and the Lies We Tell Ourselves."
10. Ettarh, "Vocational Awe and the Lies We Tell Ourselves."
11. Jean Pincott, "Silence Your Inner Critic," *Psychology Today* 52, no. 2 (2019): 48–57.
12. Amy McQueen and William M. P. Klein, "Experimental Manipulations of Self-Affirmation: A Systematic Review," *Self and Identity* 5, no. 4 (2006): 289–354.
13. Eurich, *Insight: Why We're Not as Self-Aware as We Think,* 3.
14. Tasha Eurich, "Insight Quiz," Insight, http://www.insight-book.com/default.aspx.
15. Pat Martel and Jan Perkins, "Building Career Resiliency," *Public Management* 98, no. 2 (2016): 6–9.
16. Hubert K. Rampersad, "A New Blueprint for Powerful and Authentic Personal Branding," *Performance Improvement* 47, no. 6 (2008): 34.
17. Paul S. Busch and Scott W. Davis, "Inside Out Personal Branding (IOPB): Using Gallup Clifton StrengthsFinder 2.0 and 360Reach," *Marketing Education Review* 28, no. 3 (2018): 187.
18. Gallup, "CliftonStrengths," https://www.gallupstrengthscenter.com/home/en-us.
19. Richard J. Moniz, Jr., *Practical and Effective Management of Libraries: Integrating Case Studies, General Management Theory, and Self-Understanding* (Amsterdam: Elsevier Science & Technology, 2010), 28.
20. Murray R. Barrick and Michael K. Mount, "Yes, Personality Matters: Moving on to More Important Matters," *Human Performance* 18, no. 4 (October 2005): 368.

2

Skills Development

Social skills are increasingly important to success in the workplace, libraries included. Many of these abilities are termed *soft skills* or *people skills* and may include the areas of communication, attitude, interpersonal skills, courtesy, and respectfulness. The National Association of Colleges and Employers' 2017 survey found the top skills desired by employers to be "problem-solving skills, ability to work in a team, communications skills (written), leadership, strong work ethic, analytical/quantitative skills, and communication skills (verbal)."[1] Another study of ninety business executives ranked integrity and communication as essential employee skills, followed by courtesy, responsibility, and interpersonal skills.[2] The importance of these skills is also noted in the United Kingdom's 2017 study of its workforce which cited a lack of soft skills in the workplace, including self-management, motivating staff, influencing others, and customer service skills.[3] Many of the critical skills discussed in this chapter focus on the areas of interpersonal communication, the art of conversation, and assertiveness.

Interpersonal Communication

Interpersonal communication is often intertwined with the term *soft skills* by various authors. However, in this book interpersonal communication is viewed as just one aspect of soft skills, and more specifically, as the interactions and communications between coworkers. This form of communication might encompass personality, likeability, and helpfulness. It also involves understanding the emotion or motivation of someone else in a communication exchange and being able to adjust one's own communication style as appropriate. Interpersonal communication essentially consists of getting along with others in the workplace. Karl Albrecht, the author of *Social Intelligence* (2005), says that "the ability to get along well with others and to get them to cooperate with you" exists on a spectrum from lacking (which is "toxic") to present (which is "nourishing").[4] Because libraries are close communities of teams and collaborators and often have shared workspaces for their staff, good interpersonal communication becomes essential in a functional library organization.

One method of improving our interpersonal skills in the library workplace is through multi-source feedback, also known as 360-degree feedback. As mentioned in chapter 1, this is feedback received in the workplace from supervisors, peers, and subordinates and takes the form of their responses to open-ended questions or to a rating scale. In addition to the online options previously mentioned, this method can also be facilitated at work by a human resources representative or training staff member. If there is a way for coworkers to deliver the feedback anonymously, there is a better chance the information will be accurate, since workers may not feel threatened by a fear of retaliation for something they write. Additionally, 360-degree feedback is best used as a developmental tool rather than for annual evaluations, where ratings become a game of "impression management" rather than real change.[5] Once the individual receives feedback, a plan for improvement should be established and implemented, either by the individual or by a coach, in order for real change to take place.

Related to the 360-degree feedback method is peer-to-peer feedback, in which coworkers provide feedback and constructive criticism to each other regarding work tasks or behavior. This method has been shown to have some positive impact as long as the learning level of the peers is similar. For example, it would be challenging for a new circulation staff member to evaluate a ten-year veteran's interactions with customers at the circulation desk, or for someone from technical services to evaluate a liaison librarian's interactions during an information literacy session.

SAMPLE OF 360-DEGREE OPEN-ENDED QUESTIONS

1. Based on your experiences, how does [insert name] contribute to the library?
2. What does he/she do exceptionally well?
3. What could he/she do to make the library team more successful?
4. What suggestions do you have so [insert name] can more successfully communicate in the library workplace?
5. What do you perceive as his/her greatest challenges?
6. What should [insert name] stop doing in the workplace?
7. What advice would you give [insert name]?

But if the learning levels are similar, peer-to-peer feedback can often lead to greater understanding, broader perspectives, and reflective thinking.[6] For example, library liaisons at Rollins College were evaluated by faculty members, and as a result of reviewing their strengths and weaknesses, they created a two-year plan for improving their liaison interactions.[7] However, some challenges remain with this method as to how to standardize this type of feedback and how to eliminate its possible negative psychological impact. As with 360-degree feedback, if the feedback is not anonymous, there can remain a fear of reprisal on the part of the assessor, as well as potential hurt feelings on the part of the individual who has sought feedback.[8] Additionally, there is an issue of trust, not only in one's own ability to deliver feedback, but also in the experience and knowledge of the assessor.[9]

A third method for improving interpersonal workplace communication is behavioral modeling training (BMT). BMT is a widely recognized method for successful interpersonal skills training that involves modeling proper behavior or methods in a given workplace situation. The researchers Arnold Goldstein and Melvin Sorcher developed four steps to the BMT process in 1973. These are (1) modeling or watching proper behavior in a problematic situation, (2) role-playing with a trainer to practice response skills, (3) trainer feedback in the form of praise or constructive criticism, and (4) utilizing what is learned on the job. This form of learning can also be enhanced by writing key points and mentally rehearsing the correct behaviors.[10] Of all the methods of interpersonal skill training, BMT has been shown to create a deeper level of learning that "resonates for a long time."[11] For example, a proper reference interview could be observed either live or on film, practiced behind the scenes with a coach, and then implemented at the library reference desk.

Finally, classroom-style training to improve interpersonal skills is also common. This can be a seated lecture-style classroom or a form of online training using webinars or modules. However, research is mixed on the long-term impact of this form of training. Some evidence indicates that classroom training can be effective if it is supplemented with either self-coaching or upward feedback.[12] Upward feedback, similar to 360-degree feedback, involves feedback from subordinates on behaviors, which leads to setting goals for improvement. Self-coaching is done by the individual and involves defining current behaviors before setting goals that will facilitate improvement after the class training is over. This method is typically completed with "written assessments and exercises to facilitate self-reflective and goal-setting efforts."[13]

Numerous options are available when training to improve one's individual, interpersonal skills. Whatever training technique is chosen to develop interpersonal skills, it should focus on "specific, optimal social skills, not on increased general sensitivity or insight" in order to have the most impact.[14]

Patience Leads to Successful Leadership

BRADY CROSS
Access Services Specialist,
Kimbel Library, Coastal Carolina University

I came to the library world from the private sector. I had previously worked in construction and then as a self-employed business owner for over ten years. As a result of that experience, my perception of the best workplace personality was that of command-style management rather than team leadership, since the former was more appropriate for those environments. However, the attributes of the command-style leadership personality sometimes resulted in conflict when I found myself in the library world, because I was accustomed to ensuring that project outcomes were achieved as quickly as possible. Although outcomes were achieved quickly, and with the desired result, I would sometimes unknowingly interrupt other library processes or act without considering how outcomes might affect other library projects.

My supervisors and department head did not rush to judge me because I lacked experience working inside the library environment. One of the reasons they hired me in the first place is because they recognized my diversified experience outside of librarianship. Instead, they gently let me know that I should consult my supervisor and wait for a response to ensure that all appropriate library departments had been consulted or made aware of my intentions before I took action. I learned that this is important because other library personnel have projects in the works that might be affected by my (formerly) abrupt actions.

The key quality or attribute that I needed to master in this case was patience, which is a skill I had to teach myself. It took me over a year to completely change my methods. Today, I accomplish this by purposely delaying action until I have asked myself how my actions will affect every department. I learned while practicing patience to observe other library happenings, and I also learned to respect the fact that my colleagues have priorities that might (or might not) be more important than my own. Whereas my work has always been valued, it is more respected by others now that I discuss projects with them and consider all aspects of the library before taking action. Over the course of time, I have been invited to participate in more collaborative projects that involve multiple library departments, I've become a liaison to co-curricular university departments, and have served on a statewide committee.

My supervisors have been my role models. They had the vision to see that I possessed the necessary skills for successful librarianship, and they mentored me through my early library career. They empowered me to continue providing valuable contributions to the library. I choose to lead by example and to make sure that other new library employees receive the same level of mentorship that has made my career successful.

The Art of Conversation

Conversation is an essential component of our profession. This includes conversations with patrons (either informally or in a formal reference interview), community partners, shareholders, and coworkers. Greetings and simple conversations play an important role in creating a functional library workplace. Often the lack of this informal communication is perceived as inconsiderate and distant by coworkers.

Starting conversations with coworkers can begin with a simple greeting, comment, or compliment. Asking questions also facilitates the beginning of conversations, and these questions can be closed or open-ended. However, the radio host and journalist Celeste Headlee suggests that open-ended questions are better because they force the individual to think about the question and give a more thoughtful response. Headlee relays tips for good conversations, which include finding commonalities and active listening, in her TED Talk "10 Ways to Have a Better Conversation" (www .ted.com).

Arthur C. Wassmer offers some nonverbal tips for becoming more open and welcoming as conversations begin, using the acronym SOFTEN. These include a *smile* and having an *open body and arms* (rather than a closed body posture). Lean *forward* slightly when seated, and utilize *touch*, such as a handshake, when possible. Direct *eye contact* and *nodding* to affirm that you are receiving what is being said also facilitates good communication.[15]

To keep conversations flowing, listen for keywords. These could be people, places, things, or activities which provide a topic in common that can be explored further.[16] Once a topic takes off one can ask questions, tell stories, give how-to directions, or ask opinions. Asking for examples or opportunities for follow-up questions are other methods.[17] However it is done, active listening for those essential keywords is vital.

TOPICS OF INTEREST

Books	Travel	School	Pets	Cooking
Movies	Home	Music	Family	Fashion
Science	Gardening	Fitness	Sports	Technology

SOURCE: Don Gabor, *How to Start a Conversation and Make Friends* (New York: Simon & Schuster, 2011), 64.

Ending the conversation is the final step in the exchange. This is done with a closing statement which may repeat something they said, or by a statement such as "I'll talk to you later" or "Thanks for sharing your story," along with goodbye if one is leaving the office or building.

Assertiveness

As discussed in our book *The Dysfunctional Library: Challenges and Solutions to Workplace Relationships*, one of the barriers to successful communication in the workplace could be "communication apprehension." James McCroskey originated this term in the late 1970s, and he defined it as a fear or anxiety associated with communicating with another individual or group.[18] Many times this communication anxiety occurs in those with

ARE YOU ASSERTIVE?

Try taking "The Assertiveness Inventory" by Robert E. Alberti and Michael L. Emmons, and posted by the University of New Hampshire (www.unh.edu).

an introverted personality, and approximately 20–23 percent of librarians consider themselves to be introverts.[19] One way to counter this and improve communication is through assertiveness.

Assertiveness is a type of behavior that falls between passive and aggressive behavior and involves "expressing ideas, feelings, and boundaries while respecting others' rights, maintaining positive affect in the receiver, and considering the potential consequences of the expression."[20] While the researcher Joseph Wolpe used assertiveness training to treat anxiety disorders, the crossover into the communication discipline came in 1976 with the work of Robert Norton and Barbara Warnick, who determined that assertive communication was positively associated with behaviors of talkativeness and good communication style.[21] More recently, numerous studies have pointed to the importance of assertiveness for effective organizational communication, and the need for leaders to assertively evaluate their employees.[22]

PLACES TO PRACTICE CONVERSATION

- Meetups
- Serving on committees
- Social events
- Conferences
- Networking events

Diving in Head First to a New Career Expanding Horizons

VALERIE FREEMAN, Instruction Librarian,
Johnson & Wales University Library,
Charlotte, North Carolina

When I graduated with my master's degree in library and information studies, my first professional director urged me to join a local library association. It would help me network, learn the ropes, and learn about the professional development side of librarianship. Because it was a local professional organization that was running at minimum board size at the time, they didn't have anyone volunteer to run for vice president at the end of the year, so with less than a year of board experience, I found myself volunteering.

At the time, the vice president was responsible for four professional events during the year, including a day-long conference. To be sure, the planning for these was done in groups, but the vice president took the lead. This involved engaging in discussions to decide which events would best engage area librarians, followed by asking professionals to lead those events and finding locations to hold those events.

After taking the vice president position I also was required to take the president position the following year, as well as the immediate past president position the third year. The president runs the meetings, controls the direction of the organization other than the events, has the power to appoint board members, and that sort of thing. The immediate past president has the responsibility of running elections at the end of the calendar year.

These experiences have been eye-opening and professionally strengthening for me. Before these positions, I had never had much experience with event planning, which I have since found hugely helpful in my career. Networking, too, helps to build those relationships that are so important to librarians across the board. Perhaps most importantly, the experiences helped me develop confidence as a professional librarian, explore new things, teach information literacy, build relationships with faculty, and so much more. I have learned to speak in front of people as well as how to run meetings of my peers or even superiors, which is entirely different than running a classroom. Being in an executive position on the board means that I often make it to most of the events, which is good for one's professional development.

I have been on the board for many years now, and have served in many different capacities. Integrating these skills into one's professional life is ultimately the most important element of the process. I have developed the skills and courage over the years to try many new things and propose taking the board in new directions. Sometimes these have been successful and sometimes not, but new paths often need to be explored.

Assertive behavior can provide a positive workplace dynamic and involves both a mental process and physical components. The researcher Arnold Lazarus separated the mental process into "rejecting demands, request[ing] favors," and the "initiation, continuation, and conclusion" of conversations. He defined the behavioral components as good eye contact, tone of voice (not too soft or too harsh), posture (respectful, not intimidating), facial expressions, message timing, and content (brief and direct).[23] Additionally, empathy, such as a positive comment or an understanding statement, can also be a component of the conversation and is suggested for long-term work relationships.[24]

Assertive communication is demonstrated through a method presented by Catherine Sheldrick Ross and Kirsti Nilsen in *Communicating Professionally, A How-to-Do-It Manual for Librarians* for changing others' workplace behaviors. Ross and Nilsen sug-

> ### ASSERTIVE BEHAVIORS
>
> ■ Making requests
> ■ Refusing requests
> ■ Expressing opinions/rights
> ■ Expressing feelings
> ■ Communicating positive or negative ideas
> ■ Starting/continuing/stopping conversations
>
> SOURCE: Tessa Pfafman, "Assertiveness," in *Encyclopedia of Personality and Individual Differences*, ed. V. Zeigler-Hill and T. K. Shackelford (New York: Springer International Publishing, 2017), 3.

gest using the DESC technique. The first step is to *describe* the unacceptable behavior, and the second step is to *express* how it makes you feel. This is followed by *specifying* the change(s) that you would like to see happen. The final step is explaining the good *consequences* that result from action.[25] A DESC scenario could involve a worker who is disengaged in a meeting and focused on a cell phone rather than participating. A team leader may say the following: "I notice that you're monitoring your cell phone during our event planning meeting. This is frustrating for me because I don't have your input on this important event. In the future, cell phones will not be allowed during our meetings. If everyone is focused, engaged, and contributing we will have a much better program for our customers."

A final suggestion encompasses seven steps that align with the acronym ASERTIV. These steps start with capturing the *attention* of the recipient of the communication. Second, briefly describe the *situation* with specifics. The third step is to convey the *emotional* impact of the action (or lack of action), followed by one's *reaction* or personal feeling. The fifth step is to *test* the concern level by engaging in talk about a solution. Next, *solicit* involvement in the solution and monitor progress. Finally, thank the individual and show the *value* in the new method, solution, or behavior.[26] This method may be communicated this way. "Excuse me, John, could I speak to you for a moment? I noticed the laptops were left out on the cart last night instead of being locked and recharged in their storage bin. I was surprised when I found that this morning, and I'm very concerned about both security and battery loss for the next day's use. How did that happen? Is there some way we can create a reminder so the laptops are put up nightly?" Hopefully this conversation would end up with a viable solution, upon which the leader would thank John for his assistance and cooperation with resolving the issue.

ASSERTIVE PRACTICE

Think of a scenario where you disagree with something someone did.

- Define the problem concisely.
- Using an "I" statement, express how this makes you feel.
- State what change you would like to see happen.
- Formulate a question you would ask to solve the problem and reach a resolution.

Conclusion

Interactions with coworkers and staff are a component of every library worker's day. And if these interactions are handled correctly, they can contribute to the positive dynamics of the library team and group culture. Individuals can gain a better understanding of interactions at work through 360-degree feedback, peer-to-peer feedback, behavioral management training, or classroom training. Along with this understanding comes the ability to have simple conversations with staff, not only about work but also about other topics. This adds to the human element of the work group and gives everyone a better understanding of each other as

---

QUESTIONS FOR DISCUSSION

- How well do I get along with my coworkers?
- How do my interpersonal communication skills impact the work environment?
- Do I take time to say hello and have conversations with coworkers?
- Am I able to implement assertive communication when required at work?

people, not just as workers. Finally, assertive techniques can enable individuals to address issues or problems in a logical way so as to change behaviors or actions and reach a positive resolution.

NOTES

1. National Association of Colleges and Employers, "The Key Attributes Employers Seek on Students' Resumes," November 30, 2017, https://www.naceweb.org/about-us/press/2017/the-key-attributes-employers-seek-on-students-resumes/.
2. Marcel M. Robles, "Executive Perceptions of the Top 10 Soft Skills Needed in Today's Workplace," *Business Communication Quarterly* (December 2012): 455.
3. Mark Winterbotham et al., "UK Employer Skills Survey 2017 Research Report," IFF Research, August 2018, 48.
4. Karl Albrecht, *Social Intelligence: The New Science of Success* (San Francisco: Jossey-Bass, 2006), xiii–xiv.
5. Bart Craig and Kelly Hannum, "Research Update: 360-Degree Performance Assessment," *Consulting Psychology Journal Practice and Research* 58, no. 2 (2003): 122.
6. Yu-Hui Ching and Yu-Change Hsu, "Earners' Interpersonal Beliefs and Generated Feedback in an Online Role-Playing Peer-Feedback Activity: An Exploratory Study," *International Review of Research in Open and Distributed Learning* 17, no. 2 (2006): 106.
7. Jonathan Miller, "A Method for Evaluating Library Liaison Activities in Small Academic Libraries," *Faculty Publications* 72 (2014), https://scholarship.rollins.edu/cgi/viewcontent.cgi?article=1170&context=as_facpub.
8. Ching and Hsu, "Earners' Interpersonal Beliefs and Generated Feedback," 107.
9. Roy Ballantyne, Karen Hughes, and Aliisa Mylonas, "Developing Procedures for Implementing Peer Assessment in Large Classes Using an Action Research Process," *Assessment and Evaluation in Higher Education* 27, no. 5 (May 2010): 429.
10. Phillip J. Decker, "The Enhancement of Behavior Modeling Training of Supervisory Skills by the Inclusion of Retention Processes," *Personnel Psychology* 35, no. 2 (June 1982): 323–32.
11. Ching and Hsu, "Earners' Interpersonal Beliefs and Generated Feedback," 105–22.
12. Michael J. Tews and J. Bruce Tracey, "An Empirical Examination of Post-Training on-the-Job Supplements for Enhancing the Effectiveness of Interpersonal Skills Training," Cornell University, School of Hotel Administration, http://scholarship.sha.cornell.edu/articles/938.
13. Barbara A. Sen, "Reflective Writing: A Management Skill, *Library Management* 31, no. 1–2 (2010): 79–93.
14. Cameron Klein, Renee E. DeRouin, and Eduardo Salas, "Uncovering Workplace Interpersonal Skills: A Review, Framework, and Research Agenda," in *International Review of Industrial and Organizational Psychology,* vol. 21, ed. G. P. Hodgkinson and J. K. Ford (New York: Wiley & Sons, 2006), 80–126, esp. 109.
15. Arthur C. Wassmer, *Making Contact: A Guide to Overcoming Shyness* (New York: Dial, 1978), 223.
16. Don Gabor, *How to Start a Conversation and Make Friends* (New York: Simon & Schuster, 2011), 35.

17. Gabor, *How to Start a Conversation and Make Friends*, 36.
18. James C. McCroskey, "Oral Communication Apprehension: A Summary of Recent Theory and Research," *Human Communication Research* 4, no. 1 (1977): 79.
19. J. M. Williamson, Anne E. Pemberton, and J. W. Lounsbry, "Personality Traits of Individuals in Different Specialties of Librarianship," *Journal of Documentation* 64, no. 2 (2008): 281.
20. Tessa Pfafman, "Assertiveness," in *Encyclopedia of Personality and Individual Differences*, ed. V. Zeigler-Hill and T. K. Shackelford (New York: Springer International Publishing, 2017).
21. Joseph Wolpe, *Psychotherapy by Reciprocal Inhibition* (Stanford, CA: Stanford University Press, 1958); Robert Norton and Barbara Warnick, "Assertiveness as a Communication Construct," *Human Communication Research* 3, no. 1 (September 1976): 62–66, https://doi.org/10.1111/j.1468-2958.1976.tb00504.x.
22. Ivelina Peneva and Stoil Mavrodiev, "A Historical Approach to Assertiveness," *Psychological Thought* 6, no. 1: 17–18.
23. Maria Daniela Pipas and Mohammad Jaradat, "Assertive Communication Skills," *Annales Universitatis Apulensis Seris Oeconomica* 12, no. 2 (2010): 651.
24. Pfafman, "Assertiveness," 4.
25. Catherine Sheldrick Ross and Kirsti Nilsen, *Communicating Professionally: A How-to-Do-It Manual,* 3rd Ed. (Chicago: Neal-Schuman, 2013), 51.
26. Pipas and Jaradat, "Assertive Communication Skills," 655.

3

Productive Communication

Communication is often the key to solving many problems in the library workplace. According to Shawn Long and Laura Vaughan, all communication involves the following components: sender, channel, message, receiver, noise, and feedback.[1]

Through a process referred to as encoding, communication first involves a sender encoding information, typically to inform or persuade. On the surface, this seems pretty straightforward. In practice, however, the encoding process entails our conveying information or, according to Deborah Barrett, conveying meaning, based on *all* of one's past experiences.[2] The sender's message has embedded within it assumptions that are relative to their view of the world. Just think of how potentially different one's own life experiences may be from those of others.

The next layer in the process is the channel by which information is conveyed. For example, is the information being provided face-to-face, in a meeting, through an asynchronous communication tool, through e-mail or a discussion board, or by phone? Each of these channels has pros and cons, and this has important implications.

The third layer is the receiver. The receiver has his or her own life experiences, and these will impact the process of decoding the transmitted information. According to Judith Gordon, "A receiver who has a similar frame of reference to that of the sender will experience less difficulty in decoding than one whose frame of reference differs considerably."[3] For example, communicating across cultures can be especially challenging.

Noise is another important consideration. Noise can literally mean noise! Perhaps a message is being conveyed to someone with a motorcycle rushing by in the background, for instance. Noise, though, can mean a whole lot more than that. According to Long and Vaughan, "Noise related to differences in perception can also interfere with the ability of communicators to relay a message. This type of noise is attributed to a number of factors, including non-verbal communication and cultural differences. Differences in perception can lead to conflict among the communicators."[4]

> **BASIC ELEMENTS OF COMMUNICATION**
>
> - Sender
> - Encoding
> - Channel
> - Message
> - Noise
> - Receiver
> - Decoding
> - Feedback

Lastly, feedback closes the loop. It involves acknowledgment or additional communication from the receiver. This can be an iterative process as the receiver becomes the sender and new information is processed back and forth.

Face-to-Face Communication

Face-to-face (F2F) communication is still considered the preferred means of communication in most circumstances. One study indicated that 75 percent of business executives preferred face-to-face communication over all other forms.[5] Similarly, according to extensive research on workplace communication by Stephan Braun et al., "Employees want to communicate mostly via face-to-face with their leaders, and even though leaders use face-to-face communication most often, employees still express a desire for an even more frequent use of this channel."[6] It should also be noted that certain situations are seen as more deserving of this form of communication. According to a study by Kupritz and Cowell, "Private, confidential issues, including human resource annual reviews, discipline, and promotions, elicited the most frequent responses from participants when asked to identify critical work situations requiring face-to-face communication."[7] Carol Goman reports "that 87 percent of professionals think that face-to-face meetings are essential for sealing a business deal, while 95 percent said they are the key to successful, long lasting business relationships."[8] Clearly, staff are looking to have more, not less F2F communication, and yet much of the communication in our libraries takes place through other means.

An important question to ask is why people often prefer F2F interactions in the workplace not just with a supervisor, but with peers as well. Braun et al. posit that this is due to the ability to incorporate body language and tone.[9] Goman states: "We get most of the message (and all of the emotional nuance behind the words) from vocal tone, pacing, facial expressions and body language. And we rely on immediate feedback—the instantaneous responses of others—to help us gauge how well our ideas are being accepted."[10] It can also be helpful to increase bonding if the F2F communication involves teams.

The way in which workspaces are set up can have an impact on interaction as well. At least one study highlights the critical importance of office layout to facilitate more in-person communication. Stryker and Santoro note: "Our study suggests that providing spaces for informal and formal collaboration opportunity also has the potential to facilitate increased F2F communication."[11] This has implications when designing the workspaces in our libraries or redesigning spaces that already exist.

Meetings: Considerations and Solutions

Meetings between three or more individuals constitute a significant amount of the communication that occurs in our libraries. While meetings can now occur without the participants inhabiting the same physical space, the traditional face-to-face meeting will be discussed here. In-person meetings allow for nonverbal communication which can lead to a greater shared understanding and purpose. Books such as *Death by Meeting: A Leadership Fable . . . about Solving the Most Painful Problem in Business* (2004) by Patrick Lencioni, however, are not uncommon and can conjure up some of the most unproductive moments in our library workplace. There are various examples of this. The first and foremost is when a meeting takes place for its own sake. Most everyone, at some point in their career, has attended a meeting where the information discussed could have been shared by e-mail. This is evident when a meeting involves no meaningful back-and-forth among participants. Another example is when there is no clear reason or mandate for the meeting to begin with. For example, if the committee's leader is given no purpose or direction, no real authority, and no budget to work with, these meetings may quickly devolve into a waste of time. Other ways that meetings can derail is when key members are absent or too many people in the meeting have no connection to the items being discussed. Some simple solutions for meetings are to have a clear agenda, make sure participation is widespread, and the appropriate people are included.

Communicating with Staff

REBECCA FREEMAN, Associate Librarian,
Medford Library, University of South Carolina Lancaster

I am one of two librarians in a small rural academic library. Our staff are all temporary, are primarily students, and staffing is complicated by the fact that there is no director and the students do not directly report to either librarian except for their daily tasks. I am responsible for many of the tasks that are assigned to our staff. Our library is small enough that we have our temporary staff doing a variety of jobs that would typically be handled by either librarians or full-time paraprofessionals, and they do not have a set of tasks that are done every day. Communication with our staff is vital for the efficient running of the library.

To make sure that everyone had something to do in the library on a daily basis, I had to speak directly with each individual to give them their task for that day. We have a small temporary staff, so in theory this should have worked well, and it ensured that I would answer any questions which my staff might have. The process fell flat, however, when I was on a different work schedule from a staff member or when I was out of the library. I had to rely on letting my colleague know what I needed a staff member to do, and then my colleague would pass that information on or e-mail the staff member directly to give them their tasks. Doing this was ripe with the potential of something being miscommunicated or missed. This all came to a head when I was going to be out of the library for more than a week and the staff had to do a variety of tasks in the library during this time.

In a small library there is no need to go through a committee to change how a process is done. With the problem I have described, I knew that I needed a process which did not require staff members to check their e-mail each day. I needed a solution that was cheap and could grow and change as needed. We concluded that we needed the equivalent of whiteboards for my colleague and I to write out the daily tasks for each staff member. Our solution was to create whiteboards with colored paper and page protectors. Each staff member has their own makeshift whiteboard.

This solution was cheap and easy and better streamlined our communication with our staff members. It enables our staff to come in and know what is expected from them that day, and it enables them to take responsibility for their work.

E-Mail: Considerations and Solutions

As described succinctly by one source, "e-mail serves as an effective way to send one-way messages or engage in two-way interaction that doesn't have time urgency."[12] E-mail also allows the use of broader teams over a larger area. Those of us in larger libraries or systems can appreciate its value here. E-mail's big disadvantage, of course, comes from lacking the aforementioned benefits of F2F interactions. E-mail does not allow us to convey tone, body language, or the ability to perceive how a message is received. A couple of warnings with regard to e-mail will be useful here. We should be careful about sending an e-mail when emotions are high. If we are sending an e-mail that has emotional content, it can be helpful to let it sit as a draft while we consider how the message may be decoded or received. Another obvious circumstance where e-mail can be ineffective is when the issue requires more discussion. There are some exceptions to this, however, when dealing with a larger work team and trying to keep other library staff "in the loop." Tips for success in using e-mail include being as clear, direct, and succinct as possible and including all appropriate parties. When responding to an e-mail, consider whether "reply all" is necessary.

Videoconferencing: Dimensions and Solutions

Videoconferencing is becoming increasingly common in business, library, and education-related communication. Its advantages are obvious. Communication can occur in real time across distances and is convenient. Videoconferencing is typically much cheaper than F2F communication, especially where travel may be involved, and it retains the ability to partially relay body language and tone of voice. However, it does miss some of the nuances of F2F meetings. Some tips for using videoconferencing include testing equipment ahead of time and investing in a high-quality camera and headset.

Communication Solutions Focused on Face-to-Face Interaction

Civility in all communication is critical, and is not optional for any library that wants positive interactions between staff, leadership, and patrons. Leaders in particular must model appropriate behavior and insist on civility. While other individuals in the library can play unofficial leadership roles, the formal leader's impact can be profound. A variety of other elements can help a leader establish healthy communication as well. According to Brian Appleton, some key components include setting standards, modeling, encouraging feedback, and emphasizing common goals.[13] Trust is also critical. Trust is built up over time between the leaders and others within the organization. However, it can very quickly be destroyed.

Speak the truth. It seems almost too obvious to state, but high-quality communication based on mutual trust depends on honesty and frankness. The bestselling book *Crucial Conversations: Tools for Talking When Stakes Are High* (2002) owes its widespread popularity to the fact that individuals often shy away from conversations or communications that address real problems. Civility cannot be maintained at the expense of honesty. A common concern is when no one on the staff feels brave enough to raise difficult issues. Nothing can impair the culture of an organization more than trying to gloss over problems.

Be consistent. This goes along with speaking the truth, but it also speaks to adhering to personal values even when it is difficult to do so. Everyone has heard of tailoring messages for a given crowd. Politicians do this all the time. The important thing to note is that while the emphasis may change according to our audience, the basic facts and core values should remain the same.

Beyond the issues of trust and civility, other elements make up good communication. The most important skill that can be applied by anyone is listening. According to Michael Hoppe, this involves a variety of elements such as paying attention, suspending judgment, and reflecting, clarifying, summarizing, and sharing.[14]

Paying attention involves some key elements to consider whenever one communicates. First of all, we need to be in a receptive frame of mind. Most people are thinking about the next thing they will say instead of really listening to the other person. This holds true for one-to-one discussions as well as meetings. If you need to remember some point to be brought up in a meeting, a good tip is to jot down a note so that it can be brought up later. It is also very important to show open and welcoming body language. Most people have been in many a meeting where people are not looking at the speaker, or they're even busy texting. Just stop! Besides being rude, these people cannot possibly be taking in the information being shared. Likewise, it is worth noticing the speaker's body language as well. This will help you to understand the speaker's points of emphasis.

Suspending judgment can also be tricky when actively listening. We should practice empathy and remember that everyone has a different point of view. Individuals should be patient and try to view things from a different perspective.

Reflecting and clarifying should occur as we seek to understand the points being made and try to gain further understanding on any points which were not clear. Again, many of us jump right into what we want to say without listening first. Reflecting and clarifying are especially important when we are having difficult conversations. According to Piyush Patel, people should "embrace uncomfortable conversations. When people are passionate about their work, you can't avoid uncomfortable conversations. They're a part of the workplace. Instead of trying to avoid them at all costs, embrace these conversations as a way to enhance productivity."[15]

Conclusion

Communication is a challenge in any library or organization. If individuals can be more fully aware and present when interacting with others, communication can be greatly improved. Conversations are not always easy, but they are important for resolving issues, getting to know our colleagues, and having a rich and enjoyable personal work experience. All of these things contribute to the success of our libraries. Taking the time to really listen to those we work with is the most critical element in this regard.

QUESTIONS FOR DISCUSSION

- What are your preferred means of communicating in your library workplace?

- What methods do your colleagues seem to prefer?

- How observant are you of the total message you are receiving when you interact with colleagues (e.g., body language)?

- How well do you listen?

- How can you improve your listening skills?

- How can you help your team or colleagues improve their listening skills?

NOTES

1. Shawn D. Long and Laura Vaughan, "Interpersonal Communication," in *Encyclopedia of Industrial and Organizational Psychology*, ed. Steven G. Rogelbert (Los Angeles: Sage, 2007).
2. Deborah J. Barrett, "Strong Communication Skills a Must for Today's Leaders," *Handbook of Business Strategy* 7, no. 1 (2006): 385–90.
3. Judith R. Gordon, *Organizational Behavior: An Organizational Approach* (Upper Saddle River, NJ: Prentice Hall, 2002).
4. Long and Vaughan, "Interpersonal Communication."
5. "In-Person Communication Is Most Effective," *OfficePro* 67, no. 8 (2007): 8.
6. Stephan Braun et al., "Emails from the Boss—Curse or Blessing? Relations between Communication Channels, Leader Evaluation, and Employees' Attitudes," *International Journal of Business Communication* 56, no. 1 (January 2019): 72.
7. Virginia W. Kupritz and Eva Cowell, "Productive Management Communication," *Journal of Business Communication* 48, no. 1 (January 2011): 54–82.
8. Carol Kinsey Goman, "What's So Great about Face-To-Face?" *Communication World* 28, no. 3 (May 2011): 38.
9. Braun et al., "Emails from the Boss," 73.
10. Goman, "What's So Great about Face-To-Face?" 38.
11. James B. Stryker and Michael D. Santoro, "Facilitating Face-to-Face Communication in High-Tech Teams," *Research Technology Management* 55, no. 1 (January 2012): 56.
12. Neil Kokemuller, "The Impact of Email in the Workplace," Chron, http://work.chron.com/impact-email-workplace-7915.html.
13. Brian Appleton, "7 Techniques That Work for Improving Communication in the Workplace," Envision Creative, last modified October 24, 2017, https://www.envision-creative.com/improving-workplace-communication/.
14. Michael Hoppe, *Active Listening: Improve Your Ability to Listen and Lead* (Greensboro, NC: Center for Creative Leadership, 2007), 6.
15. Piyush Patel, "10 Tips for Having a Difficult Conversation," *Public Management* 100, no. 5 (June 2018): 30.

Navigate Conflict

Conflict and dysfunction occur in the library workplace. In an original study by the authors, interaction with coworkers, with its implied potential for conflict, ranked as the second-highest stressor in the library work environment (with workload ranking as the highest stressor).[1] Additionally, another study conducted by the authors in 2017 indicated that 53 percent of all library workplaces are perceived as dysfunctional by employees, with poor communication being one of the primary causes.[2] Much of this poor communication involves one-on-one interactions between employees. This chapter will provide some basic steps for working through a minor disagreement. It will also provide some guidance for those experiencing a more toxic environment, such as bullying, and will review confronting, avoiding, reporting, and self-care behaviors for dealing with this.

One-to-One Resolution

While one-to-one resolution will not work in all situations, many minor disagreements can be handled this way. This method is defined as a "one-to-one dispute resolution . . . that involves two employees resolving their dispute through face-to-face communication and without direct intervention by management."[3] The first to explore this area of conflict resolution was Roger Fisher and William Ury. Their Model of Principled Negotiation, introduced in 1991, focused on four principles. The first principle is to separate yourself from the problem by limiting your emotional response, not taking it personally, and attempting to see the opposite point of view. The second principle involves discussing positions and exploring why each party retains their viewpoint. This includes talk about potential solutions. The third step is for both parties to creatively explore all possible solutions and shared interests in order to come to a solution that may benefit both. Finally, the resolution that is reached should be based on practical and objective criteria.[4]

In 1992 Dudley Weeks wrote a classic book, *The Eight Essential Steps to Conflict Resolution: Preserving Relationships at Work, at Home, and in the Community*. He advanced views similar to those of Fisher and Ury in emphasizing understanding each other's viewpoints and looking for win-win agreements.[5] Weeks goes on to conclude that taking the view of both parties, rather than of just one individual, can contribute positively to the resolution of the conflict. Once this is reached, actionable steps should be laid out for both parties to proceed.

More recent research has yielded other conflict resolution models which focus on the relational and skill aspects of the interaction, and moving beyond the simple step-by-step guides of early researchers. However, for this brief treatment, the simple commonalities of the models will suffice. Initially, disagreements may involve a cooling-off period if they are emotionally charged. Afterwards, a meeting between the two parties should be scheduled at which they begin to talk about their viewpoints and the issue at hand. All perspectives should be objectively discussed and common grounds determined. Then, both parties should move toward potential solutions together, rather than one individual dominating in a "my way only" attitude.

While many policy guidelines for library employees only provide information on formal grievance processes, there are some examples of one-to-one resolution steps found in the academic setting. At the University of California at San Diego, faculty and staff guidelines suggest these steps:

1. Talk with the other person
2. Focus on behavior and events, not on personalities

3. Listen carefully

4. Identify points of agreement and disagreement

5. Prioritize the areas of conflict

6. Develop a plan to work on each conflict

7. Follow through on your plan

8. Build on your success[6]

Vancouver Island University suggests a similar approach for its employees to use in direct discussions:

1. Don't talk to your colleague in anger

2. Analyze and think about the problem (not the person)

3. Set time to have a discussion

4. Communicate effectively

5. Be ready to listen

6. Work together to solve the problem

7. Keep the matter confidential

8. Keep working at it[7]

Both of these lists reiterate the importance of disengaging from emotion in face-to-face communications, and listening to both sides before developing ideas that move toward a resolution.

ELI GOLDRATT'S EVAPORATING CLOUD

When no common ground is found between two parties, try these steps:

1. Define what each person wants (side A and side B).

2. Determine what is needed to satisfy both views.

3. Find a common objective to meet both of these needs.

SOURCE: Mahesh Gupta, Lynn Boyd, and Frank Kuzmits, "The Evaporating Cloud: A Tool for Resolving Workplace Conflict," *International Journal of Conflict Management* 22, no. 4 (2011): 399.

Confronting the Instigator

Research by the authors indicates that 40 percent of library workers experience bullying and 17 percent are victims of mobbing.[8] Other recent studies found the library staff bullying rate to be 40 percent for academic librarians and 46 percent across all types of libraries.[9] These types of behaviors can be among the most toxic in the library workplace. When dealing with these difficult interpersonal conflicts, three options are typically available: confrontation, avoidance, or reporting. Confrontation is defined as assertively addressing the improper behavior and taking active steps to stop it, as described below. Avoidance involves finding ways to evade dealing with the instigator. Reporting involves a formal complaint filed through a manager or the human resources department. While this chapter will discuss all three approaches, from an individual perspective, confrontation is often (although not always) the best option. Research has shown this method to be more effective than avoidance and, due to the lack of action from human resources departments (discussed later in this chapter), reporting as well. Assertive confrontation is not only an effective strategy, but it also empowers the targeted individual and enables the development of resilience.[10]

To understand how the confronting or assertive method is effective, some insight into the mindset of a workplace bully is helpful. Bullies can take the form of openly aggressive or covertly aggressive individuals. In survival mode, their workplace mindset is an unconscious dynamic of a "life and death" feeling which "goes awry."[11] These individuals are set on doing whatever they can to set up their victims for failure. Covert bullies operate under the guise of a "pleasant employee" when there is also another, darker side that sets up more stealth-like attacks which inflict "emotional suffering before making the 'kill.'"[12] Sometimes bullying behavior is based on envy of the "goodness in others" which they desire, and once the bully feels like they have obtained their "perceived goodness" they care little "for the fate of the victim."[13] This partly explains why good library employees often become the target of a bully. Other times, bullies simply lack empathy, and the emotions of victims have no meaning or impact on them. They want to find ways to hate their targets, which "creates a distance" between them and makes it easier to view people as "object[s] to be used and abused."[14]

Given the psychology of bullies, there are assertive actions a targeted individual can take which may help. First, the target must respond to the bullying immediately and not wait until the behavior has been repeated again and again with the hope that it will eventually stop. Second, when a bully attacks, the victim can either state that it is not the right time for the discussion and leave to gather herself for an assertive talk later, or she can "maintain an assertive stance and eye contact" and deliver a counter-message right then and there.[15] Third, during the actual rebuttal the targeted individual must stick to the facts and be void of emotion beyond maintaining an assertive firmness. The target should listen to what the bully is saying for clues to that person's feelings, but should consistently draw boundaries defining their own position.

The psychologist and author Aryanne Oade provides some clear steps to take when conversing with a bully. First, whenever possible, plan the conversation in advance. The discussion will be challenging, and the bully will push back verbally, so be as prepared as possible. When talking to the bully, clearly point out what he or she is saying or doing that is offensive. Give examples of this or state your observations. (But remember, do not reveal the emotional impact being felt, since bullies lack empathy.) Be ready for the counterargument, since the bully will try to create mental confusion. Do not fall into a pattern of talking in circles with the bully, since this derails the fact statements and the focus of the conversation. Repeat the facts again if necessary, stay focused, and maintain positive, confident body language throughout the exchange.[16]

PREVENTING UNWANTED REPETITIVE EPISODES IN WORK CONVERSATIONS

1. State (repeat) the other person's view or idea.
2. Point out the problem that is directly related to that view.
3. Come to agreement on that problem and its impact.
4. Link new information and ideas to resolving the problem.

SOURCE: Janel Anderson, "Unwanted Repetitive Patterns," Working Conversations, last updated February 13, 2017, http://workingconversations.com/tag/dysfunctional-communication/.

Avoiding the Instigator

While assertive confrontation may be the best response in many instances, such as when dealing with a toxic coworker, avoidance is another option that is chosen by many people. Avoidance is an action that "involves running away . . . rather than confronting" the aggressive behavior.[17] Keep in mind that both avoidance and refusing to do anything are viewed as nonproductive because the root cause of the toxic behavior is not being addressed. Additionally, a 2016 study shows that the avoidance method decreased job satisfaction and psychological well-being, and a lack of action also resulted in poorer psychological well-being.[18]

Avoidance is chosen by many workers who fear formal reprimand, retaliation, or job loss if they confront a toxic supervisor in an assertive manner. Since 30 percent of bullying in libraries comes from supervisors, it is understandable why this method is often selected.[19] In a study of retaliation methods used by bullied workers, Pamela Lutgen-Sandvik writes the following of those targeted by a bully: "They want change but get punished; they report abuse but are stigmatized for reporting; they fight back and are labeled insubordinate. The inherent risk is why most resistance is covert."[20] Additionally, targeted workers who are hoping the behavior will eventually dissipate may start with an avoidance approach to the situation before trying more assertive actions. Several studies indicate that bullied targets are more likely to opt for avoidance, while those not directly targeted by the bully opt for other strategies, such as confronting the instigator.[21] The Workplace Bullying Institute's 2017 survey across a variety of work organizations found that 40 percent of workers did nothing when bullied, and another 13 percent of workers chose consciously to avoid the bully.[22] With over half of workers opting for these passive choices, it is apparent that this method of handling conflict is still being used by many workers who are caught up in these toxic situations.

Reporting Incidents

A third option open to individuals dealing with conflict is reporting events to human resources. Ideally this approach would lead to the resolution of the situation, but quite often this simply does not happen. Human resource specialists are not always trained in how to handle toxic workplace complaints. Additionally, these staff members tend to try to protect the interests of the organization rather than those of any one individual, so many of their actions reflect that stance.

Human resource practices can be divided into a "hard" or "soft" stance. The "hard" stance sees employees as numbers or resources to support the organization's objectives.[23] According to this stance, library employees are viewed as an impersonal resource who simply fill various roles to achieve the library's mission statement. By contrast, the "soft" stance of human resources sees employees as valuable assets who are "proactive and resourceful rather than passive inputs."[24] Happily, this latter view often predominates in libraries because they are professional organizations which are committed to the work of helping others. Sometimes, under this guise of professionalism, the organization, however, is simply getting employees to comply when they actually may retain more cynical views regarding the role of human resources. It is this way that many human resource departments fluctuate between the hard and soft models of operation.

Statistics and research points to only limited success with individuals who choose the reporting route. A 2011 study from the United Kingdom indicated that only 23 percent of harassment or bullying cases were upheld.[25] The Workplace Bullying Institute's 2017 survey across various work organizations found that only 18 percent of complaints were formally filed, and of these, the employer did nothing or there was no change in 46 percent of the cases. This means that reporting toxic behavior to human resources resulted in a positive outcome only about 10 percent of the time. Sometimes human resources may be hindered by a lack of organizational policy or training on handling these types of cases. Other times, as stated already, their loyalty lies in supporting the organization over an individual. Unfortunately, often human resource actions are simply sham investigations which give a worker lip service but ultimately delay a resolution, even disbelieving or blaming the victim for the incidents.[26]

Despite the low chance of a positive outcome, should an individual choose to report conflict and a toxic environment to the human resources department, there are several steps in the process. First, documentation is essential. One must keep detailed records of incidents, conversations, actions, and dates when filing a formal report. When addressing human resources, the report should be in concise, story-like format which contains a clear beginning, middle, and end. Next, the story should focus on the instigator and their actions rather than on the personal impact or feelings the targeted worker is experiencing. Convey specific details on occurrences of the bullying. Acknowledge other perspectives, but anticipate counter-views in advance of the human resources meeting and be prepared with what to say when alternative views come up. Additional tips include using examples which resonate with the listener, referring to others who have experienced similar conflicts, and stating the negative impacts on both peers and workplace productivity.[27] Utilizing coworker cases can bring creditability to individual claims, since a "collective voice" minimizes the chances of the targeted individual being labeled as a problem worker.[28]

Despite the limitations to reporting conflict, this is still an option that is open to library employees. However, workers should be aware that there may be negative consequences associated with this method. In addition to the possibility that no action or change will occur, there is also a chance that such action will result in a worse work environment. Toxic behaviors may increase after a formal complaint is lodged and the instigator is not stopped. Ultimately, a lack of resolution after a formal complaint fails may result in the targeted individual leaving the organization.

Self-Care

The importance of self-care when dealing with conflict and toxic work situations cannot be overlooked. While self-care actions do not address the situation itself, they can provide some relief to the target. These methods may include utilizing health services, implementing mindful releases, and sharing experiences.

Nearly all library organizations have some type of mental health service for employees as part of their health care package. This may be helpful to employees because toxic work environments cause real physical and emotional challenges in workers, including feelings of low self-esteem, depression, and anger.[29] The prevalence and impact of low morale in library workplaces was well documented by Kaetrena Davis Kendrick in a 2017 study of academic librarians.[30] Other research has shown incivility to trigger anxiety and depression as well as increased heart rate and blood pressure, migraines, ulcers, and heart disease.[31] Seeking professional help through the employee's health care services can provide some insight and suggestions for managing these issues. Examples of less formal avenues for mental health assistance can come through electronic discussion boards and social media. The annual LIS Mental Health Week in February draws attention to these needs of library workers. Its Twitter feed is #lismentalhealth, and an anonymous relay is also available for user discussions which may provide some help and guidance. Additionally, Facebook pages for librarians provide posts of shared information on both mindfulness (Mindfulness for Librarians) and managing low morale (Renewers: Recovering from Low Morale in American Libraries).

Mindful practices are another option in self-care. These range from participating in various forms of meditation, yoga, or tai chi to reduce stress and improve resilience to simpler forms such as mindful walking. The benefits of mindful practice and its practical implications for the profession have been explored in detail in a book by the authors, *The Mindful Librarian: Connecting the Practice of Mindfulness to Librarianship* (2015). One should also consider taking planned breaks during the workday and not overcommitting to projects in the day or week. Other practices include spending some time in nature and including some form of exercise in weekly routine. Many find daily journaling a safe and positive outlet to reduce stress. One should also pay attention to self-judging thoughts and recognize these as simply thoughts, and commit to actively listening to friends, family, and coworkers.[32] All of these suggestions will help reduce stress and are a form of mindful self-care.

Lastly, talking with friends and colleagues about the work environment can help. Sharing experiences and finding support keeps the library worker from feeling isolated and can make a positive difference.[33] Moreover, talking with someone who has experienced a similar work environment may also provide some emotional support.[34] However, keep in mind that replaying distressing events can bring back the negative emotion of the event. So while talking about distressing work situations is helpful, one should find a balance between sharing concerns and reliving those situations. A more in-depth discussion on self-care can be found in the next chapter.

Conclusion

All librarians experience conflict in the library workplace at some point in time to varying degrees. On an individual basis, many of these situations can be resolved through conversation. The one-to-one approach of talking it out can often bring resolution to minor disagreements. More toxic situations often push workers toward other choices, such as confronting an instigator in an assertive manner or avoiding him or her in the future. Often, when a toxic situation remains unresolved, individuals feel compelled to report the situation to the human resources department in a more formal manner. Whatever the approach, individuals must always remember self-care and embrace the support of family and friends until the situation changes or they are able to leave the organization.

QUESTIONS FOR DISCUSSION

- What kinds of resolution styles have I used in the workplace?
- What are the steps to take if I decide to confront a toxic instigator?
- What are the potential negative repercussions when pursuing resolution to a toxic work environment?
- Do I take time out to practice self-care on a regular basis?

NOTES

1. Richard Moniz, Jo Henry, Joe Eshleman, Lisa Moniz, and Howard Slutzky, "Stressors and Librarians: How Mindfulness Can Help," *College & Research Libraries News* 77, no. 11 (2016): 535.
2. Jo Henry, Joe Eshleman, Rebecca Croxton, and Richard Moniz, "Incivility and Dysfunction in the Library Workplace: Perceptions and Feedback from the Field," *Journal of Library Administration* 58, no. 2 (2018): 137, 140.
3. Fodhla McGrane, John Wilson, and Tommy Cammock, "Leading Employees in One-to-One Dispute Resolution," *Leadership & Organization Development Journal* 26, no. 3 (2005): 265.
4. Roger Fisher, William L. Ury, and Bruce Patton, *Getting to Yes: Negotiating Agreement without Giving In* (New York: Penguin Books, 1991).
5. Dudley Weeks, *The Eight Essential Steps to Conflict Resolution: Preserving Relationships at Work, at Home, and in the Community* (New York: TarcherPerigee-Penguin Books, 1994), 71, 90, 224.
6. UC San Diego, Blink, "How to Handle Workplace Conflict," last updated January 5, 2018, https://blink.ucsd.edu/HR/supervising/conflict/handle. html#5.-Prioritize-the-areas-of-conf.
7. Vancouver Island University, Administration, "Direct Discussion—How to Approach a Co-Worker," https://adm.viu.ca/workplace-conflict/direct-discussion -how-approach-co-worker.
8. Henry et al., "Incivility and Dysfunction in the Library Workplace," 137, 140.
9. Shin Freedman and Dawn Vreven, "Workplace Incivility and Bullying in the Library: Perception or Reality?" *College & Research Libraries* 77, no. 6 (November 2016): 743; Hak Joon Kim, Carole Anne Gear, and Arlene Bielefield, "Bullying in the Library Workplace," *Library Leadership and Management* 32, no. 2 (2018): 5.
10. Colleen Bernstein and Leanne Trimm, "The Impact of Workplace Bullying on Individual Wellbeing: The Moderating Role of Coping," *SA Journal of Human Resource Management* 14, no. 1 (2016): 7.
11. Sheila White, *An Introduction to the Psychodynamics of Workplace Bullying* (London: Routledge, 2018), 39.
12. White, *Introduction to the Psychodynamics of Workplace Bullying*, 39, 45.
13. White, *Introduction to the Psychodynamics of Workplace Bullying*, 39–40.
14. White, *Introduction to the Psychodynamics of Workplace Bullying*, 39.
15. White, *Introduction to the Psychodynamics of Workplace Bullying*, 43.
16. White, *Introduction to the Psychodynamics of Workplace Bullying*, 45.
17. Bernstein and Trimm, "Impact of Workplace Bullying on Individual Wellbeing," 3.
18. Bernstein and Trimm, "Impact of Workplace Bullying on Individual Wellbeing," 4–5.
19. Henry et al., "Incivility and Dysfunction in the Library Workplace," 138.
20. Pamela Lutgen-Sandvik, "Take This Job and . . .: Quitting and Other Forms of Resistance to Workplace Bullying," *Communication Monographs* 73, no. 4 (2006): 425.
21. Isil Karatuna, "Targets' Coping with Workplace Bullying: A Qualitative Study," *Qualitative Research in Organizations and Management: An International Journal* 10, no. 1 (2015): 22.
22. Gary Namie, "2017 WBI U.S. Workplace Bullying Survey," Workplace Bullying Institute, https://workplacebullying.org/multi/pdf/2017/2017-WBI-US-Survey.pdf.

23. Premilla D'Cruz and Ernesto Noronha, "Protecting My Interests: HRM and Targets' Coping with Workplace Bullying," *The Qualitative Report* 15, no. 3 (May 2010): 509.

24. D'Cruz and Noronha, "Protecting My Interests," 510.

25. White, *Introduction to the Psychodynamics of Workplace Bullying*, 10.

26. D'Cruz and Noronha, "Protecting My Interests."

27. Pamela Lutgen-Sandvik and Sarah J. Tracy, "Answering Five Key Questions about Workplace Bullying: How Communication Scholarship Provides Thought Leadership for Transforming Abuse at Work," *Management Communication Quarterly* 26, no. 1 (February 2012): 35.

28. Lutgen-Sandvik and Tracy, "Answering Five Key Questions about Workplace Bullying," 36.

29. P. M. Forni, *The Civility Solution: What to Do When People Are Rude* (New York: St. Martin's Press, 2008), 13

30. Kaetrena Davis Kendrick, "The Low Morale Experience of Academic Librarians: A Phenomenological Study," *Journal of Library Administration* 57, no. 8 (2017).

31. Sandy Lim, Lilia M. Cortina, and Vicki J. Magley, "Personal and Workgroup Incivility: Impact on Work and Health Outcomes, *Journal of Applied Psychology* 93, no. 1 (2008): 98.

32. Richard Moniz, Joe Eshleman, Jo Henry, Howard Slutzky, and Lisa Moniz, *The Mindful Librarian: Connecting the Practice of Librarianship to Mindfulness* (Waltham, MA: Chandos, 2015), 22–23.

33. Lutgen-Sandvik and Tracy, "Answering Five Key Questions about Workplace Bullying," 37.

34. Maria Grazia Cassilto, *Raising Awareness of Psychological Harassment at Work* (Albany, NY: World Health Organization, 2002).

5

Wellness and Self-Care

S elf-care is often a neglected consideration when exploring healthy workplace environments and interactions. Ironically, it is when one feels most unable to dedicate time to wellness and self-care that it is needed the most. In a study which covered 629 library staff from 44 states and 5 countries, the following were the top overall stressors:

38% — Workload and time management

14% — Colleagues

9% — Instructional workload

8% — Patrons

7% — Short deadlines

7% — Administrators[1]

Kevin Harwell has highlighted the prevalence of work overload as a major stressor in libraries, as well as the ability, or rather inability, to craft one's role.[2] Karen Jensen has pointed out the stress associated with problem patrons and the anxiety in school libraries associated with active shooter drills.[3] Additional issues include bullying, harassment, mobbing, and a lack of general civility in the workplace.

In addition to the stressors listed above, librarians are experiencing rapid change in the field such as new resources and services being provided, how work is structured, evolving roles, and fund allocation (which often means having to do more with less). No type of library is immune from these developments. Often, library workers do not take the time to take care of themselves and are impacted by "vocational awe." As defined previously in this text, "'vocational awe' refers to the set of ideas, values, and assumptions librarians have about themselves and the profession that result in the belief that libraries as institutions are inherently good and sacred, and therefore beyond critique."[4] One consequence is that librarians often emphasize self-sacrifice as an ideal. It is good to be dedicated, but this can translate into their putting their own personal well-being far behind that of those they serve.

According to one author who has explored burnout among physicians, "To combat provider burnout, a cultural shift must be undertaken by the entire system. It must be aimed at improving the daily lives of providers. By fostering a culture that recognizes the potential of burnout and teaches providers about it, burnout might be avoided."[5] Likewise, another recent study indicated that job satisfaction and employee retention can be positively influenced by workplace wellness programs.[6] These statements could apply equally well to librarians. While all employees may not be in danger of burnout, everyone faces stressors which can impact their well-being, as well as their overall effectiveness and the capacity to perform to the best of their ability. Employers should be taking deliberate steps to improve employee wellness and stave off burnout. Leaders have a key role in this regard. That said, sometimes these efforts may need to be undertaken on an individual or piecemeal basis.

Exercise and Job Performance

According to a recent study on promoting exercise and physical fitness, "Implementing physical activity interventions in the workplace seems to be an effective way to prevent burnout and promote vigor among employees."[7] While this study encouraged regular walking, a wide variety of other promising approaches also exist to promote physical fitness. According to Bhibha Das et al., "only about 20% of Americans meet both aerobic and muscle-strengthening PA [physical activity] and public health guidelines."[8] This is an obvious opportunity in a profession such as ours where most employees are sedentary for much of the day.

There are many examples of workplace wellness programs. One program entitled "Fit From Your Desk" encourages employees to engage in regular stretches and physical activity right in their workspaces.[9] Horry-Georgetown Technical College, likewise, provides instruction for staff on exercises that they can do at their desks. One study, which encouraged the use of lunch and break times to engage in physical activity, discovered that "self-directed exercise—especially that which fits into a typical one-hour lunch break—was associated with important mood benefits. Second, performance increments consistently favored the exercise condition. Third, exercising was associated with a wide range of beneficially changed work attitudes and perspectives regarding self, tasks and colleagues."[10] Yet another study in Finland recently concluded:

> A 12-month physical exercise intervention had a clear impact on the well-being of the working adults. Stress symptoms of the exercise group decreased and mental resources, leisure time physical activity, as well as cardiorespiratory fitness improved during the 12-month intervention, and these positive changes remained after the follow-up year. The improvements were the greatest among the persons who at the baseline had the most stress symptoms and the least mental resources.[11]

One of the more creative attempts to influence not just library staff but also the communities they serve is the website and organization "Let's Move in Libraries." Created by the library educator Noah Lenstra, the project's mission is as follows:

> The Let's Move in Libraries project focuses on supporting health and wellness with physical activity in public libraries. The project was inspired by Former First Lady Michelle Obama's Let's Move! initiative, which focused on increasing physical activity and healthy living among Americans. Mrs. Obama worked to increase physical activity through museums. We continue her legacy by working to increase physical activity through libraries in the U.S., Canada, and other places in the world.[12]

For library leaders, encouraging physical activity in a formal program or even informally can be constructive. One study determined that greater physical activity was related to "better mental well-being and work performance."[13] One should create a wellness plan to incorporate various levels of exercise in the daily routine.

Mindfulness

Mindfulness is a broad concept that encompasses a variety of practices or ways of being. It focuses on awareness of the present moment and treating ourselves with patience and kindness. Research indicates that nearly 80 percent of library staff have engaged in mindful practices of some kind, and approximately one-quarter of library staff engage in mindful practice on a regular basis.[14] Mindfulness can encompass meditation, yoga, mindful eating, mindful walking, and tai chi, to name just a few examples.

One common introduction to mindfulness is the eight-week Mindfulness-Based Stress Reduction (MBSR) course pioneered by Jon Kabat-Zinn at the University of Massachusetts, and now widely available throughout the United States. This inclusive approach introduces participants to a variety of mindful practices. A recent study which implemented a six-week version of MBSR suggests that "six weeks of mindfulness-based skills training can result in reductions in perceived stress among a diverse paraprofessional workforce working in environments of urban poverty."[15] MBSR has the most significant impact on those professions with the greatest stress. It is no longer uncommon for police officers, for example, to be provided with a course in MBSR. One recent study indicated that "in post-training surveys, participants reported feeling less burned out and better equipped to deal with stressful situations, both at work and at home. They also felt a heightened state of awareness when awake and consistently logged longer, higher-quality periods of sleep."[16] In fact, MBSR has proven useful in even the *most* extreme cases of stress, such as PTSD. Kyle Stephenson et al., after studying the use of MBSR with veterans suffering from PTSD, concluded that their "study provides the first fine-grained examination of the association between changes in mindfulness and PTSD symptoms using a large sample of veterans with clinically relevant PTSD symptoms undergoing an empirically supported mindfulness-based intervention."[17] It is no surprise, then, that librarians are interested in mindfulness. The book *Recipes for Mindfulness in Your Library: Supporting Resilience and Community Engagement* (2019) points to a wide variety of ways that libraries are engaging staff and patrons in these types of activities.

Labyrinths and Libraries:
Take a Walk on the Winding Side

MADELEINE CHARNEY, Research and Liaison Services Librarian,
W. E. B. Du Bois Library, University of Massachusetts Amherst

My story begins in 2014, when the UMass Amherst nursing professor Donna Zucker set up a projected labyrinth at the W. E. B. Du Bois Library (where I work in Research Services). Intrigued, I volunteered to walk the labyrinth as a subject in her study on stress reduction. It turned out that the Sparq labyrinth she used was invented by a librarian, Matt Cook, from the University of Oklahoma. More intrigue ensued.

My participation in Dr. Zucker's labyrinth study opened up a door for me professionally and personally. I began reading and seeking out labyrinths in my area to walk, learning that these structures date back to the Neolithic period and appear around the world. Though sometimes confused with a maze, which has dead ends, a labyrinth is in fact a single path—one way in, one way out. According to the World Wide Labyrinth Locator (https://labyrinthlocator .com/), there are currently almost 5,000 labyrinths in 80 countries.

Staying in touch, I mentioned to Dr. Zucker that I was helping plan a mindfulness retreat for library staff in the Five College Libraries consortium. She told me of a colleague, a nurse at the local county jail, who had a 25' × 25' foldout canvas labyrinth that she might be willing to lend me. When this turned out to be the case, the rest of the retreat planning team was enthusiastic about adding a labyrinth walk to the day's offerings. It was exciting to try something new, and it was gratifying to see the calming effect on library staff who chose to walk the labyrinth (our feedback survey showed it as the most popular offering). After that, I longed to have a labyrinth on hand for future offerings to library professionals,

A few months later, I did a presentation on librarianship and mindfulness at the conference of the Association of Mental Health Librarians. I was new to the group, and was glad to join their ranks. Looking at their website one day, I noticed a link to their Small Grants Program and an idea popped into my head—a proposal for a canvas labyrinth to be used exclusively with library professionals. The group generously granted me $1,400, and I gleefully awaited the arrival of my 16' × 16' version from the Labyrinth Company.

My first foray with this labyrinth was at the New England Library Association conference in Burlington, Vermont. It was a fun task to scope out just the right spot in the conference center and then invite attendees to give the labyrinth a try. I posted the spot on Twitter, and also stopped attendees as they bustled between sessions, meals, and meetings. Most of them looked at me quizzically; walking a labyrinth is not your typical invitation at a conference. However, many reported how it boosted their conference experience. For example, it helped ease some people down from a presentation they had just delivered and calmed others before presenting.

Before people entered, I explained how labyrinth walking can decrease stress and also aid in concentration, increase creativity, or help you find a hidden answer to a difficult question. I discreetly observed many of the walkers pausing in the center of the labyrinth before retracing their steps, lifting arms up high, and taking a few deep breaths—truly using the moment to recenter themselves. Back home in western Massachusetts, I also brought the labyrinth to a local college library, setting up for two hours in the mid-afternoon. I captured some of their comments after their walk:

> "The pause [in the middle] was very powerful. I've done walking meditation before, but not in a labyrinth."

> "I never realized how fast I usually walk. I've never walked so slowly, and without shoes."

> "At one point I felt panic [chuckles], like I was lost. And then I realized I'm on the same path."

> "It was like doing yoga. Sometimes I felt self-conscious. Sometimes I felt like I was walking a tightrope, then I would not notice I was walking. I was just drifting along."

Another time, I set up the labyrinth at my local public library. As I entered the building, I witnessed a challenging patron interaction. The weariness on the librarian's face was apparent. There was a bustling atmosphere and everyone, at every service point, was moving fast.

Nevertheless, many of them found their way downstairs to where I had set up the labyrinth. Their comments to me were poignant and reflective of the kind of day they were having:

> "This was the cherry on top of my day . . . You should bring this to Washington, DC."

> "We need this now." Then she pondered about building a labyrinth on the property or in a park downtown."

> "We should do this here once a month . . . our work life is so chaotic."

> "The town offers some stuff, but nothing specifically for us."

"I could really feel my feet. If I weren't on the clock, I would have gone slower."

Her: "This is a perfect day for this."

Me: "Seems like people are really frazzled here today."

Her: "It's the whole world" [shaking her head].

To bring the labyrinth experience to library colleagues near and far has brought me great joy—to support their healing, enjoyment, concentration, insights, and dreams.

Mindfulness: Meditation

Meditation is the most common mindful practice. There are many different meditation practices in use. The most common forms are breathing meditations, body scan meditations, loving-kindness meditations, and walking meditations.

Breathing meditation involves paying attention to one's breathing. While simply paying attention to one's breathing can be helpful, true breathing meditation requires that individuals find a quiet place where they will not be interrupted for a period of time. In many libraries, a designated room for meditation may exist, such as the one at the McQuade Library at Merrimack College. The staff at the McQuade Library were able to utilize grant funding to provide not just a space for meditation, but also MBSR classes.[18] Johnson & Wales University's Charlotte campus library dedicates a study room to meditation. It also sponsors meditation sessions that are open to faculty, staff, and students. Jennifer Sippel at Minneapolis College was able to repurpose an old copy machine room and brand it as a "Room to Breathe."[19] The common theme in all these efforts is to be creative.

Breathing meditation can be done in a variety of ways, but the most common method is to sit in a chair or on a meditation pillow with your hands at your side or on your lap. Next you close your eyes and pay close attention to your breathing. Most people find it helpful to use a guided breathing meditation. This could be through the use of an app such as Calm or Headspace, a live facilitator, or even a YouTube video. One YouTube video that can be good for beginners is "Guided Breathing Meditation with Kim Eng." This video provides a short, ten-minute guided breathing meditation for anyone to use to get started.[20] Even ten minutes a day of this meditation can make a difference.

Body scan meditations can also be useful. Body scan meditations are a natural outgrowth of the work of Jon Kabat-Zinn. He wanted to help patients deal with issues associated with chronic pain. Body scan meditation can do this by allowing one to consider the different sensations in one's body. This can be done sitting or lying down on a mat. The process involves moving your awareness through the different parts of your body, paying attention to any sensation found there. Most people find it helpful to have some sort of guidance in the form of a facilitator or a recording.

Loving-kindness meditation is also common. Loving-kindness has been shown to positively impact empathy. It involves repeating short mantras focused on one's self and others. For example, you might hold in awareness yourself, a loved one, or even someone you are currently at odds with and repeat phrases such as "May you be well. May you be peaceful. May you be happy." One of the best books on this topic is Kristin Neff's *Self-Compassion: Stop Beating Yourself Up and Leave Insecurity Behind* (2011).

Lastly, the formal practice of walking meditation involves walking within a small space in a deliberate fashion. As you walk, you pay attention to each movement (e.g., "I am lifting my foot. I am stepping forward," etc.). According to the *Encyclopedia of Emotion*, "walking meditation is usually practiced as a form of expanding one's attention; as the meditator walks, she attends to all stimuli external to her own thoughts or feelings— the surrounding environment, the act of walking, physical sensations of walking, and so on."[21]

Mindfulness: Yoga

One of the most common mindful practices is yoga. Yoga can take many forms but typically involves purposeful body movements using very specific postures. There are wide-ranging benefits from yoga. A recent study reported: "findings suggest that in 2 months, a weekly 60-min yoga class has demonstrated positive psychophysiological benefits for women, which may be protective of developing stress-related psychopathology."[22] For a more specific library example, one can look to Millie Jackson at the University of Alabama's University Library. Jackson brought her skills as a yoga instructor into the library to provide sessions on "restorative yoga" that were open to anyone in the community. She states: "Through the offering of Restorative Yoga, the library is becoming a place that nurtures not only the mind but also the body and spirit. Restorative Yoga offers a space for relaxation and relief from stress and tension."[23] Since there are so many different approaches to yoga that target different age groups and abilities, it is very important to explore your options here.

Nature

Spending time in nature seems to be a remedy for many of us. A recent study of military veterans who were engaged in white-water rafting found that they experienced a boost in well-being. The study's conclusion states: "For John Muir, the outdoors were a source of both restoration and awe. In the current study, we captured both these properties of nature experience, showing for the first time that awe mediates the effect of nature experience on well-being. These findings suggest that awe may be one active ingredient in the remedy that is time spent outdoors."[24] Another study "confirmed the hypothesized increase of feelings of restoration, vitality, and positive mood in green environments and their decrease in a built urban setting. In addition, feelings of creativity were higher in green environments. The findings of the study also confirmed that experiential restoration can take place after a short period of nature exposure."[25] Spending time in nature can also reduce high cortisol levels. In a study lasting 8 months, subjects were asked to spend at least 10 minutes "in nature" at least 3 times a week. Their cortisol levels were then measured against a control group. Those who regularly spent 20–30 minutes in nature experienced the greatest reduction in stress hormone levels.[26]

Job Crafting

The control one has over one's job is also worth consideration. Having more control over one's daily tasks can have a significant impact on stress reduction. Numerous studies have pointed to job crafting as a way to reduce stress and engage employees. One study stated: "Our findings support many previous studies that have demonstrated that work engagement and job crafting are strongly related to each other."[27] Another qualitative study went a step further, stating: "Organizations should stimulate job crafting, and especially the seeking resources strategies. Such strategies have beneficial effects on task performance and altruism. This means that similar to the suggestion of earlier research on proactivity, empowering individuals to make work their own and in accordance with their needs and preferences can increase effective behavior."[28]

The critical element in the above examples is the ability of a person to craft his or her job. What both research and personal intuition tell us is that employees who can craft at least some part of their work will tend to be more engaged. Library staff should find a way to engage in activities at work that bring joy, and which produce a great sense of internal motivation. In some cases, this may require that individuals speak to a supervisor and discuss ways to craft their job as such.

Professional Development

As a staff member, one should seek out professional development as well when considering well-being. If the library lacks funds for this, it may be up to the individual to determine what is or is not feasible. Engaging in continual learning is critical for our overall well-being.

There is much evidence to connect the idea of professional development with improved morale and well-being. In addition to Martin House's research, for example, Jennifer Gore et al. found that providing teachers with professional development improved both the quality of their teaching and their morale.[29] Another study which explored teacher morale determined that teachers with access to greater professional development opportunities were retained at a higher rate.[30] Likewise, Brenda Simon notes that "employee training programs lead to increased job satisfaction and higher employee performance."[31] Individuals should be learning all the time. Ideally, that learning should be as self-directed as possible.

> **GET CREATIVE WITH PROFESSIONAL DEVELOPMENT**
>
> - Participate in free webinars.
> - Find an informal mentor.
> - Get involved in a local library association.
> - Read ALA books.
> - Read library blogs.

Reframing and Moving On

One of the most difficult things to do for self-care is to know when to try something different in one's job, or just move on. Sometimes an organization can be large enough for an individual to simply move into a different area of the library or take on new roles. At other times, the growth opportunities are limited. Unfortunately, some unsatisfactory workplace situations just cannot be fixed. This is a very hard conclusion to reach for many staffers. But sometimes self-care requires a plan for moving on. Often, even just having a plan can help with one's well-being.

Conclusion

Librarians are dedicated in the service they provide. In doing so, however, they may not always take into account their own needs. There are many ways to remedy this. Exercise, mindfulness activities such as meditation and yoga, mindful walking, and spending time in nature can all contribute to well-being. Other practical solutions can include job crafting, professional development, and seeking new roles at work. In some cases, an individual may decide they need to move onto something new. Lastly, while not discussed in this chapter, you should not rule out the value of using counseling through the library's Employee Assistance Plan. The value of having an objective, third-party person help you explore and talk through individual situations should not be underestimated.

QUESTIONS FOR DISCUSSION

- How well am I doing in taking care of myself and my needs at work?
- What new activities or approaches could help me reduce stress and become more engaged in my library?
- How can I develop a personal wellness plan?
- What makes me most excited and happy in my library job? Can I do more of this?
- Am I happy in my current role in my library? If not, what can I do about it?

NOTES

1. Richard Moniz et al., *The Mindful Librarian: Connecting the Practice of Mindfulness to Librarianship* (Waltham, MA: Chandos, 2016).

2. Kevin Harwell, "Burnout and Job Engagement among Business Librarians," *Library Leadership & Management* 27, no. 1/2 (January 2013): 6.

3. Karen Jensen, "Framework for Managing Patron Stress," *School Library Journal* 65, no. 3 (April 2019): 17.

4. Fobazi Ettarh, "Vocational Awe and the Lies We Tell Ourselves," *In the Library with the Lead Pipe*, January 10, 2018, http://www.inthelibrarywiththeleadpipe.org/2018/vocational-awe/.

5. Matthew Michael Eschelbach, "A Proposed Review and Fix for Burnout," *Physician Leadership Journal* 5, no. 6 (November 2018): 49.

6. Stephanie Pink-Harper and Beth Rauhaus, "Examining the Impact of Federal Employee Wellness Programs and Employee Resilience in the Federal Workplace," *Journal of Health & Human Services Administration* 40, no. 3 (winter 2017): 353.

7. Clément Ginoux, Sandrine Isoard-Gautheur, and Philippe Sarrazin, "'Workplace Physical Activity Program' (WOPAP) Study Protocol: A Four-Arm Randomized Controlled Trial on Preventing Burnout and Promoting Vigor," *BMC Public Health* 19, no. 1 (March 12, 2019): 12.

8. Bhibha M. Das et al., "From Sedentary to Active: Shifting the Movement Paradigm in Workplaces," *Work* 54, no. 2 (June 2016): 486.

9. Angela Lombardi, "Employees Get Fit from Their Desks: PG&E Fitness Program Combats Risks of Prolonged Sitting," *Professional Safety* 62, no. 6 (June 2017): 70.

10. Jo C. Coulson, J. McKenna, and M. Field, "Exercising at Work and Self-Reported Work Performance," *International Journal of Workplace Health Management* 1, no. 3 (2008): 187.

11. Oili Kettunen, Timo Vuorimaa, and Tommi Vasankari, "A 12-Month Exercise Intervention Decreased Stress Symptoms and Increased Mental Resources among Working Adults - Results Perceived after a 12-Month Follow-Up," *International Journal of Occupational Medicine & Environmental Health* 28, no. 1 (January 2015): 158.

12. Noah Lenstra, Let's Move in Libraries, http://letsmovelibraries.org/about-us/.

13. Anna Puig-Ribera et al., "Self-Reported Sitting Time and Physical Activity: Interactive Associations with Mental Well-Being and Productivity in Office Employees," *BMC Public Health* 15, no. 1 (2015): 9.

14. Richard Moniz et al., "Stressors and Librarians: How Mindfulness Can Help," *College & Research Libraries News* 77, no. 11 (2016): 534.

15. Rachel Jacobs et al., "A Pilot Study of Mindfulness Skills to Reduce Stress among a Diverse Paraprofessional Workforce," *Journal of Child & Family Studies* 26, no. 9 (September 2017): 2584.

16. David Schimke, "Taking Mindfulness to the Streets," *Chronicle of Higher Education*, January 27, 2017.

17. Kyle R. Stephenson et al., "Changes in Mindfulness and Posttraumatic Stress Disorder Symptoms among Veterans Enrolled in Mindfulness-Based Stress Reduction," *Journal of Clinical Psychology* 73, no. 3 (March 2017): 214.

18. Catherine Wong, Katherine La Flamme, and Michaela Keating, "Mindful McQuade: Mindfulness in the Heart of a Small College Campus," in *Recipes for Mindfulness in*

Your Library: Supporting Resilience and Community Engagement, ed. Madeleine Charney, Jenny Colvin, and Richard Moniz (Chicago: American Library Association, 2019), 30–31.

19. Jennifer Sippel, in *Recipes for Mindfulness in Your Library: Supporting Resilience and Community Engagement,* ed. Madeleine Charney, Jenny Colvin, and Richard Moniz (Chicago: American Library Association, 2019), 92.

20. Kim Eng, "Guided Breathing Meditation with Kim Eng," YouTube video, 10:51, posted October 14, 2011, https://www.youtube.com/watch?v=67SeR3LxtdI.

21. "Meditation," in *Encyclopedia of Emotion*, ed. Gretchen M. Reevy (Westport, CT: Greenwood, 2010).

22. Kaitlin N. Harkess, Paul Delfabbro, Jane Mortimer, Zara Hannaford, and Sarah Cohen-Woods, "Brief Report on the Psychophysiological Effects of a Yoga Intervention for Chronic Stress: Preliminary Findings," *Journal of Psychophysiology* 31, no. 1 (2017): 45.

23. Millie Jackson, "Providing a Space to Rest: Weaving Restorative Yoga into the Strategic Plan," in *Recipes for Mindfulness in Your Library: Supporting Resilience and Community Engagement*, ed. Madeleine Charney, Jenny Colvin, and Richard Moniz (Chicago: American Library Association, 2019), 26.

24. Craig L. Anderson, Maria Monroy, and Dacher Keltner, "Awe in Nature Heals: Evidence from Military Veterans, at-Risk Youth, and College Students," *Emotion* 18, no. 8 (December 2018): 1201.

25. Liisa Tyrväinen et al., "The Influence of Urban Green Environments on Stress Relief Measures: A Field Experiment." *Journal of Environmental Psychology* 38 (June 2014): 8.

26. Najja Parker, "Feeling Stressed? Take a 20-Minute 'Nature Pill,' Study Says," *The Sun News,* April 19, 2019, 10A.

27. Jari J. Hakanen, Maria C. W. Peeters, and Wilmar B. Schaufeli, "Different Types of Employee Well-Being across Time and Their Relationships with Job Crafting," *Journal of Occupational Health Psychology* 23, no. 2 (April 2018): 297.

28. Evangelia Demerouti, Arnold B. Bakker, and Jonathon R. B. Halbesleben, "Productive and Counterproductive Job Crafting: A Daily Diary Study," *Journal of Occupational Health Psychology* 20, no. 4 (October 2015): 466.

29. Jennifer Gore et al., "Effects of Professional Development on the Quality of Teaching: Results from a Randomised Controlled Trial of Quality Teaching Rounds," *Teaching and Teacher Education* 68 (2017): 111.

30. Tray Geiger and Margarita Pivovarova, "The Effects of Working Conditions on Teacher Retention," *Teachers and Teaching* 24, no. 6 (2018): 625.

31. Brenda Simon, "Strategies to Reduce Employee Turnover in Clinical Logistics" (doctoral dissertation, Walden University, 2019), 95, https://scholarworks.waldenu .edu/cgi/viewcontent.cgi?article=7951&context=dissertations.

PART II

The Functional Team

6

Team Formation

Often library teams are created in a direct, organized manner, while at other times, these teams come about organically and occasionally are composed voluntarily. Each design can lead to teams that from the start are not unified or directed and do not make a real difference. How can library workers be more proactive and focused in order to create cohesive and effective teams? One can begin by reflecting on what it means when a group of people is declared a "library team." Certainly, the word *team* often refers to members on the same side during a game or sporting event, yet in a business or educational workplace sense the term refers to "a group of people with different skills and different tasks, who work together on a common project, service, or goal, with a meshing of functions and mutual support."[1] A team is different from a random group, and in essence it works collectively to achieve something. Most libraries have missions or vision statements, so it could be quite easy to state something like "our library team works collectively to support student success, and meet the needs of our community" (or whatever the case may be). Of note here is the replacement of the word *library* by the words *library team*. This change alone may be a bigger factor than you might think.

The choice of words and the connotations of those words are often overlooked. Although it may appear to be quite trivial, replacing the word *library* with *library team* in our oral and written communication may have a much larger effect than we might think. While the phrase *library team* creates a shared sense of purpose and unity, it also replaces the concept of "library as building" with "library as a group of people" in a similar way that "community college" elevates the term "college." Perhaps intentionally using *library team* whenever referring to library staff and leaving the word *library* to refer to the physical building and space could be of great service. Additionally, making a concerted effort to gently admonish those outside of the library to try and do the same could create a better realization of how these terms differ. It also has the added advantage of taking the word *librarians* out of the hierarchy of internal library discussions which may leave other library workers feeling excluded or marginalized.

In addition to making a concerted effort to boost the concept of a library team at every opportunity, there is also the importance of showing the value and optimizing teamwork in the library. But how is this library teamwork measured and assessed? A functional library team would be one that is confident that they are consistently meeting the goals that they have created or been assigned. Assessing a team can be a way to become much more purposeful about the teamwork that is being done in your library. Good project management has built-in assessment processes, yet many libraries may not have the forethought, organizational skills, or resources to assess their team projects. Perhaps minimizing the amount of productivity (which does not have assessment built in) for a smaller number of team projects that can be assessed is a good tactic here.

Teamwork has continued to gain in importance in education, and it is the rare class that does not contain a team project or assignment. This strategy can be seen even in the earliest grades, and because of the importance of teamwork in the workplace, it makes sense to expose students to it early and often. According to Carnegie Mellon University's Eberly Center for Teaching Excellence & Educational Innovation,

> Properly structured, group projects can reinforce skills that are relevant to both group and individual work, including the ability to:

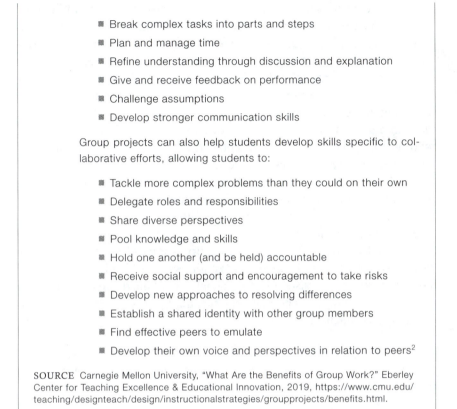

- Break complex tasks into parts and steps
- Plan and manage time
- Refine understanding through discussion and explanation
- Give and receive feedback on performance
- Challenge assumptions
- Develop stronger communication skills

Group projects can also help students develop skills specific to collaborative efforts, allowing students to:

- Tackle more complex problems than they could on their own
- Delegate roles and responsibilities
- Share diverse perspectives
- Pool knowledge and skills
- Hold one another (and be held) accountable
- Receive social support and encouragement to take risks
- Develop new approaches to resolving differences
- Establish a shared identity with other group members
- Find effective peers to emulate
- Develop their own voice and perspectives in relation to peers[2]

SOURCE Carnegie Mellon University, "What Are the Benefits of Group Work?" Eberley Center for Teaching Excellence & Educational Innovation, 2019, https://www.cmu.edu/teaching/designteach/design/instructionalstrategies/groupprojects/benefits.html.

In this chapter, the organization of a functional library team is examined, with some consideration given to how to create diverse groups, ways to utilize group dissenters, best practices around the use of teams, and how to align library teams using a shared mindset and goals. An example of organizing teams around strategic institutional goals in a library will also be offered.

Diversity of the Group

Diversity is a topic that continues to grow in importance in the library field. It has touched many aspects of librarianship, including public services, hiring, collection development, archives, digital librarianship, and of course, library management and leadership.

At the core of a move towards a more diverse workforce in libraries is the reality that librarians are overwhelmingly one race, that is, white. While there is a litany of reasons why this is bad for both libraries and society, one of the primary reasons this needs to change is because it does not reflect the communities that libraries serve. This, in turn, suggests that librarians of color are not offered opportunities in libraries, especially in leadership roles. This vicious cycle gets compounded when the field is not welcoming, comfortable, nurturing, or supportive to librarians of color, who therefore have less desire to enter it. Although the dismal numbers cited in the blog post "Lack of diversity by the numbers in librarianship and in book stuff" by Chris Bourg are ten years old, libraries have not made great strides in this area. In a follow-up post from 2014, Bourg documents in a statistical and graphical ways how skewed these numbers are in the field of librarianship.[2]

The AFL-CIO's Department for Professional Employees' *Library Professionals: Facts and Figures Fact Sheet 2019* states: "The librarian profession suffers from a persistent lack of racial and ethnic diversity that shows few signs of abating."[3] The numbers backing up this statement are quite daunting (see sidebar).

AFL-CIO Department for Professional Employees, *Library Professionals: Facts and Figures Fact Sheet 2019*:

Over 77 percent of librarians were White, non-Hispanic in 2018. Library technicians and assistants were only slightly more diverse. Among library technicians and assistants in 2018, 74.8 percent were White, non-Hispanic.

In 2018, just 6.8 percent of librarians identified as Black or African American, 8.6 percent as Hispanic or Latino, and 4.6 percent as Asian-American or Pacific Islander.

Librarians are less diverse than the total workforce of people in education, training, and library occupations. Black and African American professionals made up 10.6 percent of the education workforce, while Hispanic and Asian professionals represented 10.7 percent and 4.5 percent of the education workforce, respectively.

As has been pointed out by some astute observers of this issue, trotting out numbers is a good start to creating awareness of this issue, but are there libraries that have implemented specific procedures and programs to actively solve this problem? One example would be the creation of a devoted diversity document such as "A Framework to Foster Diversity at Penn State University Libraries' Diversity Strategic Plan 2010–2015."[4] As a way to gauge a library team's preparedness for diversity, there is the "ClimateQUAL: Organizational Climate and Diversity Assessment," designed at the University of Maryland and now run by the Association of Research Libraries.[5] One thing that seems to be lacking at this juncture is concrete examples of libraries that have attained the diversity advocated in these and other documents, which analyze the problem and strategize for its correction.

The job title "diversity librarian" (and similarly titled positions) has continued to gain traction in academic libraries. Libraries have become much more serious about grappling with the diversity problem which plagues the profession. A promising note is that as libraries become more diverse, especially in leadership positions, diversity advocates gain more power. Perhaps in our lifetime we will see (and be part of) the real changes that need to occur in the area of diversity.

Utilize a Dissenter

Each group seems to have at least one dissenter; that is, a person who is unwilling or unable to pull their fair share of the workload, one who finds a way to "game the group dynamic" to their advantage, the contrarian who seems at first to balance the group but then moves into becoming a saboteur. Although all of these do not precisely define the dissenter, these (and other) personalities appear to always be part of groupwork. As in most things, having the ability to recognize these types early on and a strategy for dealing with them can help minimize their negative impact. Quite early when writing our original book, *The Dysfunctional Library: Challenges and Solutions to Workplace Relationships*, we pinpointed communication problems at the core of dysfunction. In tandem with this idea was the realization that library workers need to self-reflect much more about why there is dysfunction in their library. In many cases, pointing out dysfunction in others (or in systems, or in other areas of the library) is often much easier than examining one's own dysfunction. In other words, are there things we may do that contribute to the library team's dysfunction and eventual breakdown? Although it can be much easier to point the finger at others and absolve ourselves of any responsibility, self-reflection on our own shortcomings can be a worthwhile exercise to engage in.

It is never easy or painless to come to terms with one's own short-comings or one's contribution to negative outcomes. The discomfort of cognitive dissonance, wherein individuals can be confronted by evidence that they are doing something harmful or negative—such as pointing out the unhealthy effects of smoking to someone who continues to smoke—is something that perhaps everyone can relate to on some level. It can be a good exercise to step back and think about the things that one considers to be dysfunctional within the library and then ask, "Do I contribute to this dysfunction in some way?" It is not difficult to place blame on others and abdicate one's role when finding fault in how things are done.

Dissenters can be helpful on occasion, especially if they offer con-structive solutions. Though complainers are often viewed negatively, there are reasons to believe that someone who complains can have a valid point or argument; too often, however, these people are quickly shut down. Sara Ahmed, the author of *Living a Feminist Life* (2017), shows how complaint sifts out the structures of institutional power. She is able to show how diversity is shut down in the same way that complaint is, and she points out "how feminist complaint can be a form of diversity work: as the work you would have to do before some populations can be included within institutions."[6] Of note here is the idea of listening and taking seriously what the dissenter says, of not initially shutting them down, and instead engaging with anyone may be making valid points about the teamwork being proposed or done. At a minimum, we should be willing to engage with the one who holds opposing viewpoints and is willing to voice them. Often the dissenter will relent or can even become a valuable team mem-ber if their ideas are listened to, so a practical solution here would be to give them a forum for their thoughts and a way to voice them. Once again, giving the member of a library team the opportunity to be heard will often be enough, even in those cases where their full grievance will not be explored.

Shared Mindset or Goal

Although there has been some solid criticism of the ideas of growth and fixed mindsets, the core of the idea still has appeal. Carol Dweck is the champion of the idea that our attitudes toward our abilities have a great impact on our achievements.[7] In a nutshell, this approach pinpoints atti-tudinal change as a leverage point for moving forward. For those who are "stuck" with thoughts that they cannot change or adapt, this type of self-fulfilling prophecy handicaps their ability to move forward. Conversely, those who posit that they can and will grow are on the correct path. Of course, there is much more to this idea, and it can easily be refuted as a type of mind trick that needs much more practical steps if real achievement is to occur. Despite the risk of trivializing the idea here, one can see the benefits of beginning at a positive place to enhance how library teamwork is thought about.

In a 2008 study that primarily addressed good assessment procedures on library teamwork, M. S. Baughman found that "there were some valuable lessons learned during this assessment project. When consulting with other libraries or searching the literature for best practices, what surfaced was that there is no one best way to approach change. Internal and external factors play roles that are not always within the control of the library's leadership."[8] This idea that external factors beyond the control of libraries affect work surely resonates with the majority of library workers (including those not considered members of the leadership). More important here is the idea that many approaches can work and often, an understanding of your institutional culture and your library team are the most important factors. When shared mindset is discussed it should be noted that in ways very close to the alignment of group behavior and a concrete team goal, each team member should have some type of mutual overlap. In chapter 14 of this book, change and resistance to new ideas and procedures are discussed. Once more, from a solutionist's point of view, how one is able to create best practices that impact the library team is less important than their implementation.

In the vignette given in this chapter, a strategic plan was developed by a library branch which set forth some focused initiatives that they wanted to achieve. This "take the situation into your own hands" approach shows the library team's intention to partner and create exact and detailed action items for their library. This approach shows how a shared mindset for a particular library can be communicated to other libraries in the system and to library leadership.

Reimagining the Strategic Plan for a Branch Library

ABBEY B. LEWIS, Interim Head,
Jerry Crail Johnson Earth Sciences & Map Library,
STEM Learning & Collections Librarian,
University of Colorado Boulder

The University Libraries at the University of Colorado Boulder developed a Strategic Plan in order to guide and coordinate their work from 2016 through 2020. The plan's goals and action items cover a wide range of library services, enhancements to organizational culture, and relationships with departments across campus, but with a document written so broadly, it was difficult for the Jerry Crail Johnson Earth Sciences & Map Library (a branch library of six employees) to see how their specific work could be recognized in the larger picture. This led to a feeling of being distanced from the libraries' efforts, and a lack of motivation to contribute to the work undertaken as part of the Strategic Plan.

In order to better facilitate its participation in the libraries' Strategic Plan, the branch set out to create its own plan, with action items and goals mapped to the larger plan. They began with a series of meetings in which they reviewed the strategic plan item by item to determine if they were already doing work that could align with the libraries' identified effort, or if they could further develop or undertake new initiatives that would coincide with the libraries' vision.

Following these brainstorming sessions, the branch worded the existing work and newly identified initiatives as action items that spoke directly to the branch's activities. The reworded action items were then grouped under new goals that read as actionable on the branch level. These new action items and goals were then mapped to the libraries' action items and goals through a table in the branch's strategic planning document.

In this way, the libraries' action item to "*Increase the libraries' involvement in curriculum development and student learning outcomes across campus by creating new partnerships, and leveraging existing expertise*" became the branch's action item, "*Explore new instruction opportunities and formats, especially those that cross disciplines.*" Similarly, the libraries' action item to "*Enhance user-centered collection development processes and data curation models that support interdisciplinary research, lifelong learning, and student success*" became the branch's action item to "*Seek direct and formal faculty input (via polls, survey, etc.) for collection development, specifically for instructional use.*"

Once written, the libraries' deans received a draft version of the plan for their approval and further input. The branch shared the finalized plan across the libraries, with particular emphasis on units which had the potential to act as partners for the branch's goals. This increased buy-in for the new plan among the branch's personnel and validated that the work they would undertake in the plan would be seen and appreciated. For the following annual evaluation cycle, branch personnel wrote personal goals that could be mapped to the branch's action items, and thereby the larger libraries' plan. Monthly one-on-one meetings between personnel and the branch head tracked progress on individual goals and created opportunities for guidance. The careful mapping of action items between the two plans assisted branch personnel and the libraries' administration with recognizing the branch's contributions to the libraries' goals.

Aligned Group Behaviors

Agreed-upon behaviors and norms are the bedrock on which many institutions function. And in their own field, libraries have shared values which help to guide many of their missions. For example, many academic libraries follow the core vision of their institutions to primarily support student success. In the public library realm, supporting the needs of the community members that use the library generally takes precedence. In fact, supporting communities could be said to be at the core of most library work, even though the tenuous connections may not always be evident.

Although sports analogies can often be overwrought and forced, when the word *team* is used, it is difficult to avoid them altogether. The idea of "team chemistry" is often brought up by sports announcers and analysts, and perhaps a look at how it is used can be helpful here. Similarly, "other factors, like how people get along together or how well they trust each other, suggest that teams are not just an aggregation of individuals and their attributes, but also the relationships that exist previously among them."[9] Team chemistry can collectively be built as a number of strong relationships that build together and align. When a team has aligned it is something to behold. Harkening back to the sports team comparison, a team that is "working on all cylinders" can be not only very productive but also rewarding for the team members. Marianne Ryan makes use of good sports/workplace comparisons in her article "Managing the Team."[10] She uses the strategies of "maintaining perspective, leading by example, and building trust" and then connects these to the methods of Joe Maddon, the Chicago Cubs manager, to show how they can apply to the library.

Of particular interest to academic libraries is a type of team that can be created through the library liaison role. Outreach teams can also occur in the public library. An interesting step in the evolution of the liaison role was a shift from subject specialists to aligning the position to be more in line with functional roles. Currently, libraries have leveraged liaison roles more aggressively towards other support groups on campus, and the collaboration angle has been even more focused upon student success. The key to all of these group formations is aligning team behavior for consistencies with the communities that libraries serve.

Conclusion

At its most basic level, this book is written to provide concrete solutions. Although some background and current thoughts and ideas on the topics at hand can be valuable, the main purpose here is to give the library strategies for dealing with the issues that they might confront and particularly those that create dysfunction in their library. As mentioned throughout the book, the examples are displayed to move the discussion along and provide concrete ideas for other libraries to consider.

Chapter 9 of *The Dysfunctional Library: Challenges and Solutions to Workplace Relationships* is entitled "Difficulties with Team Composition," and within that chapter is the idea that organizing and designing a team within the library is the most optimal way to create functional teams. Expanding on this notion and connecting it with the idea of good leadership, it appears as if there needs to be a much more dedicated initiative within many libraries to think about the teams within their purview. Ideally, this chapter with a good grounded solution can be a start to that discussion leading to action.

QUESTIONS FOR REFLECTION

- Does your library work collectively as a team? Does your department/group/committee in the library do so?
- Has your library done a diversity evaluation or undertaken any policies or actions to become more diverse?
- Has there been any discussion at your library about a strategic plan for teamwork? Do you assess the teams in your library?
- Do you think about and design teams in your library, or do you create them without goals and cohesion?

NOTES

1. Steve Holbrook, "The Responsibilities of a Teammate," 2018, http://sholbrook.com/the-responsibilities-of-a-teammate/.
2. Chris Bourg, "The Unbearable Whiteness of Librarianship," Feral Librarian, 2014, https://chrisbourg.wordpress.com/2014/03/03/the-unbearable-whiteness-of-librarianship/.
3. Department for Professional Employees, AFL-CIO, *Library Professionals: Facts & Figures Fact Sheet 2019*, 2019, https://dpeaflcio.org/programs-publications/issue-fact-sheets/library-workers-facts-figures/.
4. Penn State University Libraries, "A Framework to Foster Diversity at Penn State University Libraries' Diversity Strategic Plan 2010–2015," 2015, http://equity.psu.edu/updates-10-15/pdf/academic_frmwrkplan/framework_plan/Univ_Lib_plan_10_15.pdf.
5. Jennifer Vinopal, "The Quest for Diversity in Library Staffing: From Awareness to Action," *In the Library with the Lead Pipe*, 2016, http://equity.psu.edu/updates-10-15/pdf/academic_frmwrkplan/framework_plan/Univ_Lib_plan_10_15.pdf.
6. Stephanie Maroney, "Sara Ahmed, Complaint: Diversity Work, Feminism, Institutions," UC Davis Feminist Research Institute, 2018, https://fri.ucdavis.edu/news/sara-ahmed-complaint-diversity-work-feminism-institutions.
7. Carol Dweck, "Mindset for Achievement," Mindset, 2010, https://mindsetonline.com/howmindsetaffects/mindsetforachievement/index.html.
8. M. S. Baughman, "Assessment of Teams and Teamwork in the University of Maryland Libraries," *portal: Libraries and the Academy* 8, no. 3 (July 2008): 293–312, doi:http://dx.doi.org/10.1353/pla.0.0005, http://ezproxy.cpcc.edu/login?url=https://search.proquest.com/docview/216167025?accountid=10008.
9. Northwestern University, "In Team Sports, Chemistry Matters: Sports Analytics Analysis Reveals That Past Shared Success among Team Members Improves Odds of Future Wins," ScienceDaily, www.sciencedaily.com/releases/2018/12/181204095355.htm.
10. Marianne Ryan, "Managing the Team," *portal: Libraries and the Academy* 16, no. 2 (April 2016): 219–23, doi:http://dx.doi.org/10.1353/pla.2016.0022, http://ezproxy.cpcc.edu/login?url=https://search.proquest.com/docview/1784465332?accountid=10008.

7

Promote Communication Flow

T here are great variations in how libraries are structured and function. For example, public libraries serve a much different community than do academic or special libraries. To exaggerate this disparity, a library team worker in an urban public library may often need to perform work more akin to a social services employee or first responder, while a technical services librarian at a college may rarely communicate directly with patrons. Despite these differences, both of these library workers would still need to have excellent communication skills, including an obligation to connect consistently with their fellow employees.

Communication is a vast concept that we ask to be represented with one word. The word *communication* is often tossed out casually with little recognition of how it is being used in individual cases and how people understand it. For example, how does one assess whether there is good or bad communication within a library? Is there a general measurement or baseline for such a thing? How would you score your library regarding its functionality as it pertains to communication?

Gauging the communication environment in your library may be difficult to do. While there may be some instruments (mainly from the business world) that could lead to understanding where your library stands in this regard, there are so many singular communication instances, and attempting to freeze the communication flow is so difficult, that assessment in this arena can be a moot point. An alternative approach would be to borrow the concept of "agency" from critical librarianship, take a closer look at the power structures within your library, and analyze their relationship to communication. Because "critical librarianship seeks to be transformative, empowering, and a direct challenge to power and privilege,"[1] it sheds light on communication issues and can also hopefully begin conversations about diversity and inclusivity. While these topics are touched upon throughout his book, they are examined in more detail in chapter 13. The Brock University Library created a critical librarianship teaching toolkit[2] for its library liaisons, thereby putting a bit more teeth behind the theory. Critlib.org is a good portal for subject matter about this topic.

Communication flow should be considered a dynamic process that ideally moves in numerous directions. As open communication generally starts "from the top," library workers become more comfortable sharing information with the leadership and with each other. What does communication that "flows" look like? Like water, it should be all around and relatively accessible. In addition, it should be as "free" as possible, that is to say, in an optimized library workplace, all communication is based on trust and honesty and therefore, transparency should be a given. To say that it is not in most workplaces is a huge understatement. Not only are there silos that keep knowledge from flowing freely (more on this topic later), but there are also hierarchies that hoard information, sometimes knowingly. Often leadership is looked to for model behavior, and strong library leadership that sets an example of good communication flow is sending a strong message to their library team.

With all this said, it can be interesting to think about the way communication works within a library, and how information specialists get their own information. A common lament among knowledge workers is the overabundance and, often, the pointlessness of e-mail communication. An exaggerated response to the question "What do you do?" by some librarians is the cynical reply "My job is e-mail." Many workers have developed strategies for alleviating this e-mail glut. Workflow strategies and software solutions can allow for in-box zero cases which create efficiencies and produce less stress. Other solutions include the move to other forms of communication, such as face-to-face, which minimize e-mail use, and moving to other collaborative-focused software such as Slack, n-task, and Yammer. Of course, these tech solutions can cause new problems with every solution they offer. In one post, Joshua Kim points out that "the only problem with Slack as an e-mail replacement, and a group collaboration platform, is that Slack is now another place to go. We must check both e-mail and Slack. We get notifications that we have Slack messages and e-mail messages."[3] The main goal here is to get communication to flow freely, rather than stifle it with bad habits built within systems; this is how additional tech silos are created.

In this chapter, we will examine how communication flow could be helped by breaking down silos that close off communication, finding and leveraging those who can cross boundaries (to help obliterate those pesky silos), and then rallying library staff around clear and consistent objectives.

Prevent Silos
(Up, Down, and Lateral Communication)

Silos do not occur naturally within an organization. They can be the products of privilege, information-hoarding, power plays, and even cliques. Despite cases where those who are part of them may not consider themselves active participants, these silos are often intentional. The silos discussed here are not natural or physical barriers, but those instances where information is not shared among employees. In the current world in which we live, where communication is quite easy, silos should be a thing of the past. And yet they are not.

The different ways in which individuals or groups can cordon themselves off from others would form a large list. Certainly, forming groups is a natural tendency and should not be frowned upon. However, when people close themselves off from others due to lines drawn according to their department or division, their rank or position, or their race, gender, age, or generational affinity, this can be how silos form and harden. In libraries, there can be territorial thinking that sadly leads to division rather than cooperation. These silos can harden through the years, as expressed on this take which offers some solutions: According to Vijay Govindarajan in a *Harvard Business Review* article, organizational culture creates silos by "protecting what is rather than . . . what could be". Govindarajan recommends focusing on innovation and aligning strategic goals to "inspire people to work together" for a common goal.[4]

An exploration of any organization that has managed to avoid silos would most likely show a workplace that has grappled with its communication problems. While this issue is often raised within libraries, it is the rare library that makes a concentrated effort to alleviate silos. Similar to companies, institutions and people who say they desire to be more inclusive and diverse, when examined more closely it can be difficult to see what was implemented, monitored and assessed about those who merely discuss improving communication. Once more, because this book focuses on active solutions, shining a spotlight on some libraries that have moved beyond the discussion and theoretical phases to work to break down silos will be looked at.

The solution provided for this chapter at the Kimbel Library (see the vignette) shows how mixing various levels of expertise can break down silos and improve knowledge exchange. This type of diversity can bring up topics such as work studies in the academic library, cross-training, and onboarding. Although it seems counterintuitive at first to have another communication point to check, this case points out how a centralized communication point can improve communication flow.

An often-overlooked aspect of silos and libraries is how the library itself may create and perpetuate outward-facing silos. For example, if a library is not interacting with the community it serves, it could be said to be siloed from it. One good place to start is evaluating how your library collection conveys diversity. A recent *Library Journal* article states, "According to LJ's 2019 Public Library Diverse Materials Survey, only 9 percent of responding libraries have conducted a collection diversity audit, while another 14 percent plan to run one in the future."[5] The author Annabelle Mortensen concludes, "When it comes to diversity audits we shouldn't allow the perfect to be the enemy of the good. Any attempt to view library collections and programs through an equity lens is valuable, and any actionable data provides a foundation for developing strategies to diversify our libraries"[6]

"Karen Jensen of the Fort Worth Public Library, TX, gives a good overview of a practical application of the diversity audit in her blog post "Doing a YA Collection Diversity Audit: Understanding Your Local Community."[7] It is easy to see the amount of work it takes to perform a diversity audit of your collection, even one in a small library. However, thinking more about the community you serve and directly connecting to it through your collection seems a very worthwhile goal. A larger initiative which tries to get the word out about diversifying collections is the We Need Diverse Books program. Pointing out the value of creating a world in which we can "imagine a world in which all children can see themselves in the pages of a book," this initiative offers examples of books that promote inclusivity and more closely mirror the community the library serves. Again, when advice like this is followed, conversations begin inside and outside the library and silos are erased.

Utilize Boundary Spanners

Perhaps calling someone who is able to communicate well with a wide and diverse variety of people a "boundary spanner" is not quite accurate. Annemarie Lloyd has done a great deal of work in the field of workplace information literacy. She points out that knowing those in the workplace who have expertise in the workplace environment is a form of information literacy.[8] These people could be considered "boundary spanners" because they have the ability to communicate to a larger group than others. Often this person could be someone at the front desk, such as a receptionist or an administrative assistant, and due to the nature of their job they collect a great deal of information from a wide variety of employees in the workplace. Perhaps another term for this type of worker would be a "connector" or "conduit" who has a more holistic understanding of the workplace and can span the boundaries between different areas of the organization. It is easy to see how important it is to have library workers who understand (on multiple levels) what the library is trying to achieve. Although it would most likely be library leaders who have this capability, this may not always be the case.

It is here that library outreach comes into play, since it is a way for boundary spanners and those who function as conduits to show their value. As library work continues to move away from focusing on the physical collections in the library and toward prioritizing other services offered to the community, outreach continues to become more and more important. Promoting communication flow here is extraordinarily important because it is an opportunity to show the library's value and let your library community know what you have to offer it. R. David Lankes, in the second edition of his book *Expect More: Demanding Better Libraries for Today's Complex World* (2016), says that libraries need to embrace their outreach role and help to define and expand the role of the library. In order "to thrive, communities need libraries that go beyond bricks and mortar, and beyond books and literature. We need to expect more out of our libraries. They should be places of learning and advocates for our communities in terms of privacy, intellectual property, and economic development."[9] Taking the idea of spanning boundaries to a whole new level, Lankes shows how the community/library divide can be bridged by allowing communities to become more involved and participatory in the direction their libraries take.

Once again, the vignette for this chapter provides one nice solution to promoting communication flow, and part of that is enlisting boundary spanners. What is nice about this solution is that it is a focused initiative that uses boundary spanners, in this case, those who have the capability to work in different areas and who work as library connectors within its strategy.

Effective Departmental Communication in a Full-Service 24/7 Library

JENNIFER HUGHES, Associate University Librarian,
Coastal Carolina University

MICHELLE LEWIS, Manager of Access Services,
Coastal Carolina University

The Access Services Department of the Kimbel Library of Coastal Carolina University is comprised of 17 staff members who are responsible for service provision over three shifts, 24 hours per day, 7 days per week. All of these staff members are responsible for performing all aspects of the department, including providing reference service, processing interlibrary loans, performing circulation and stack maintenance activities, managing the facility, and supervising more than 50 student assistants. It is imperative for library users to receive consistently high levels of service provision regardless of the time of day or the day of the week, and for management of the student assistants to be continuous by a large number of supervisors. Internal communication is a tremendous challenge, especially given the fact that there are very few opportunities during the year for all staff to be scheduled for in-person meetings or trainings. Therefore, it is essential to ensure that all staff have access to necessary information in a nontraditional format.

We have found that the most effective way to create an environment of continuous internal communication is to designate an e-mail alias (i.e., a forwarding e-mail address) for the department. The staff use access@yourdomain.here to communicate all notable library transactions, and this ensures that staff members who are working different days and shifts are receiving the same information. The e-mail alias is used to relay information regarding library automated system overrides, encounters with difficult patrons, and to relay work orders submitted. Circulation notices are also sent via the access e-mail alias, so when patrons respond, the e-mail is received by all staff within the department. Staff simply "reply all" to ensure that the whole department is included in the conversation with the patron. If a staff member is trying to justify making an exception to library policy, the supervisor's response is also sent constructively via "reply all." This creates a learning moment for all employees. The supervisor may provide validation of the exception or provide additional training for all members of the department. This process gives the staff an opportunity for feedback and continuous brainstorming in order to provide the best possible solution for future issues. Additionally, if policies or procedures are altered or updated, e-mails provide documentation that can be used to update the department's official procedure manual.

The result has been one continuous online conversation, which can be extremely overwhelming in the e-mail in-box. However, it has proven time and time again to be a lifesaver. When a patron comes to the desk to follow up, they do not have to be told to come back next Tuesday during a specific shift to see the person they spoke to the previous time. Any staff member can search e-mails and be brought up to speed quickly. It has also revolutionized the way student assistants are mentored and coached. When an employee works directly with their supervisor on a regular basis it is easy to track their performance, but with so many supervisors it can be difficult to identify performance issues or track a pattern. Thanks to our system, it is easy to see that the employee has had an issue addressed multiple times by multiple supervisors. Ongoing collaborative electronic communication has fostered an environment of service excellence in our library.

Conclusion

Communication flow should be considered a process. Visualizations can often bring much-needed clarity and convey more concise information to a process than simple text. Perhaps as a start to analyzing one's library environment, it would be good practice to create process documentation and workflow documents that may affect how your library functions from day to day.

As can be seen in this chapter, evaluating the communication flow in the library can lead to innovative solutions that create learning moments and lead to time-saving procedures that are considered to be lifesavers for library staff. You should take the time in your library to reassess how you communicate, and then analyze those broken points (often created by silos) and work together to remove them. You may well find that improving the flow of communication in your library will improve efficiency, elevate employee engagement, connect you with your community, and minimize dysfunction.

QUESTIONS FOR REFLECTION

- What are the main ways the leadership communicates in your library? Is the primary way the most effective one?
- Can you identify information or communication silos in your library or institution? What are the main causes of them?
- Do you know how your job fits into your library's objectives?
- Do you think that your library would benefit from an assessment of its communication flow?

NOTES

1. Kenny Garcia, "What Is Critical Librarianship?" 2015, Association of College & Research Libraries, http://www.ala.org/acrl/publications/keeping_up_with/critlib.
2. "Critical Librarianship?" Teaching Toolkit: A Professional Development Resource for Liaison Librarians at Brock University, 2018, https://researchguides.library.brocku.ca/c.php?g=99848&p=4976000.
3. Joshua Kim, "Forced to Slack?" Inside Higher Ed, Technology and Learning, 2018, https://www.insidehighered.com/blogs/technology-and-learning/forced-slack.
4. Vijay Govindarajan, "The First Two Steps Toward Breaking Down Silos in Your Organization," *Harvard Business Review*, August 9, 2011, https://hbr.org/2011/08/the-first-two-steps-toward-breaking-down-silos.html.
5. Annabelle Mortensen, "Measuring Diversity in the Collection," *Library Journal*, 2019, https://www.libraryjournal.com/?detailStory=Measuring-Diversity-in-the-Collection.
6. Mortensen, "Measuring Diversity in the Collection."
7. Karen Jensen, "Doing a YA Collection Diversity Audit: Understanding Your Local Community (Part 1)," *School Library Journal*, 2017, http://www.teenlibrariantoolbox.com/2017/11/doing-a-diversity-audit-understanding-your-local-community/.
8. Annemarie Lloyd, "Learning to Put Out the Red Stuff: Becoming Information-Literate through Discursive Practice," *Library Quarterly* 77, no. 2 (April 2007): 181–98.
9. R. David Lankes, *Expect More: Demanding Better Libraries for Today's Complex World*, 2nd ed., 2016, https://expectmorelibrary.info/wp-content/uploads/EMSecondEdition/ExpectMore2.pdf.

8

Utilize All Communication Methods

While the topic of communication methods in libraries was explored to some degree in the previous chapter (with a focus on promoting communication flow), a detailed and holistic approach to the various methods of communication was not. Newer communication methods that elevate collaboration such as Slack and Google Drive are gaining traction, and while these types of solutions are most often used for project work, they can also be used as a way for library workers from different libraries to communicate and collaborate.

Library communication methods in a formal sense generally revolve around e-mail, meetings, a centralized space such as an intranet, and some other group activities such as retreats and team-building exercises. Often, informal communication such as impromptu meetings in offices and hallways and conversations outside the workplace can be just as valuable (if not more so) than scheduled communication events. Most of these settings are examined here (and in other chapters) in some detail, and the main thesis is that a combination of communication methods that are proven to work for libraries is most likely the avenue to walk down. It is worthwhile to note the suggestions in the previous chapter as they relate to making an intentional effort to assess and analyze the ways that one's library communicates in order to come up with evidence-based solutions to communication problems.

Meetings are often the bane of many employees' lives, and not just those working in libraries. At the core of a mismanaged or ineffectual meeting is the idea of lack of respect for the participants' time. The seemingly endless list of things that can go wrong in a meeting and actually inhibit (rather than facilitate) real communication seems to bring up the question of why meetings occur at all. Of course, the generally agreed answer to this is that meetings are one of the only formats where communication for groups can take place. Obviously, the distance and conferencing communication afforded by platforms such as Webex, Zoom, Skype, and other videoconferencing solutions helps to open the possibility for more inclusive and focused meetings. However, it can be interesting to explore a common answer to why meetings take place, which usually runs along the lines of "we have to have meetings" or "we have always had meetings."

The authors found in their previous book that many of the cases where bullying and incivility take place can occur in meetings. For example, the idea that a library employee is not heard can happen during a meeting. In chapter 14 of this book, a close examination of those who are resistant to change occurs. Within that concept, the idea of reflecting to a greater degree on how each of us contribute to dysfunction is put forth. Stepping away briefly from the common refrain of how empathy can help in situations like this, let's take a deeper dive into empathy.

Jade E. Davis has done a great deal of work deconstructing how empathy works, and she pokes some interesting holes in the idea of its value. In the same way that civility can be used to uphold systemic power hierarchies and shield people from grappling with serious issues, empathy is both a word and a concept that can be used as a convenient stopgap to real change. This can cloud and offload the real work needed. Davis says, "To the contrary, to let go of empathy is to allow a new space of meaningful and positive spaces. Rather than trying to feel the pain of others, allow space for critical or deep listening. Do not try to enter the crisis, or be the person. Instead listen, observe, be with. There is nothing special about being with another, nor is any suffering exceptional unless the work is done to make it so."[1] Once again, (similar to empty discussions around diversity and inclusion) this type of work can seem to be counterintuitive to those accustomed to a comforting emotional response as a representation of the work needed to be done to create equality.

Hopefully, the vignette in the preceding chapter about finding new ways to think about old approaches and mindsets emphasizes the idea that libraries must constantly reexamine what they do. There are many new ideas that have come to light about how library staff treat both the patrons that enter the library and each other. Concepts such as privilege, intersectionality, colonization, and critical librarianship are just a few of the ways in which library workers should reevaluate their relationships with structures and people. As one begins to learn about these ideas and grow in the course of understanding them, then some of the core values of librarianship can be fully realized.

In this chapter, in-person communication and when to use other forms of communication are discussed, as well as the ways employees prefer to get information. Lastly, how to use those communication methods wisely is explored. This includes courtesy, give-and-take, and empathy, which has already been discussed.

In-Person

It is usually a given in many cases that face-to-face communication is the best method; certainly it is the one most favored when dealing with sensitive issues or interpersonal problems. While the case can be made that there are other favorable types of communication for specific employees and situations, in-person communication is difficult to beat. One caveat here is that the quick and focused communication that technologies such as texting and e-mail can provide often surpass direct in-person communication. This aspect of the current communication streams available to employees will be discussed later in this chapter. For now, this writing will delve into why direct in-person communication can be valuable in the library.

An often overlooked opportunity within the library is consistent and well-managed one-on-one meetings. Through personal experience as a supervisor, the benefits of meeting one-on-one with staffers each month cannot be overstated. One of the many benefits of this practice is the opportunity each month to bring up a wide variety of communication: reconnecting after busy times, updates on what each employee is working on, how goals are being met (or not), how the library and the library field are doing, and any issues, challenges, and even informal topics unrelated to the job can be discussed. Once again, from a personal point of view, it seems unfathomable that fellow employees and especially those in management positions do not meet regularly. In fact, it would appear that not meeting regularly would be a strong indicator of avoidance and dysfunction.

Although he is discussing a business rather than a library environment, Michael Massari is an outspoken proponent of face-to-face encounters. He states: "face-to-face meetings are still the most effective way to capture the attention of participants, engage them in the conversation, and drive productive collaboration. If we don't continue to nurture strong and positive personal relationships with our clients and coworkers, we won't build trust, understanding, or a sense of a shared mission—all of which are critical elements to successful partnerships and business success."[2] The ability to create trust, understanding, and a sense of shared mission also helps employees to feel comfortable speaking their mind and feel that they are being listened to.

Despite the continued advance of technology into all aspects of our lives and the options new technologies give us for communicating, many still prefer face-to-face encounters. Part of their appeal is that they bring a sense of humanity to the proceedings and allow for humane interactions. While there are countless articles on the internet that point out the different ways that technology makes us less human, an interesting twist on this is the Human Library in Denmark. Working under the slogan "unjudge someone," this library checks out people *as* books. Its website sums up how this works: "The Human Library is, in the true sense of the word, a library of people. We host events where readers can borrow human beings serving as open books and have conversations they would not normally have access to. Every human book from our bookshelf represents a group in our society that is often subjected to prejudice, stigmatization, or discrimination because of their lifestyle, diagnosis, belief, disability, social status, ethnic origin, etc."[3] Although this example does put more of an emphasis on patron rather than employee relations, it provides experiences that help to achieve some of the other goals in this book: initiating in-person discussions, improving listening skills, learning about others, and understanding the various lives within our communities.

When to Use Other Forms of Communication

In libraries, there is a great desire to create banks of information resources, such as FAQs (Frequently Asked Questions) and other information repositories, in order to facilitate communication and help both patrons and staff find specific information, procedures, and answers. While these are obviously valuable, it can be difficult to gauge if they are always used efficiently and effectively. Alluded to in chapter 11 is the idea that each staff member bears some responsibility for keeping up with information about the library. This responsibility is generally not taken very seriously, however. Perhaps to give this idea some "teeth," there should be some questioning when a staffer comments about missing some type of information that is internal to the library. Questions put forth to those who miss communication could include "What are the steps that you took to attempt to find the information previous to the situation where the information was not relayed?" and "What are some of the reasons in relation to your responsibilities that the information was not communicated?" The key issue here is getting everyone to realize that information-sharing works both ways.

E-mail as a form of communication has been delved into here, as well as face-to-face connections. What are some of the other ways that librarians receive information? Gossip was a topic in *The Dysfunctional Library: Challenges and Solutions to Workplace Relationships,* and among the interesting points made about it was that gossip can be valuable because it can create shared norms (of course, there are negative effects too) and that policies which seek to eliminate gossip are unlawful.[4] Moreover, informal communication and learning can be just as effective as that done in formal spaces. Public libraries have been at the forefront of creating informal learning spaces such as makerspaces, new technology areas such as video and audio studios, and gaming areas, as well as designing spaces for specific age groups to interact. The outreach and communication opportunities that these spaces create are invaluable.

Many libraries attempt to use a centralized communication portal such as an intranet. In some cases, they provide a common area or a website that facilitates information flow. How and when these shared communication spaces are used is important. There is, of course, the problem of information glut, a situation where employees don't see the point in constantly checking for communication missives that do not apply to them. A similar problem arises with e-mail. The low-level whiteboard solution profiled in the vignette in chapter 3, "Communicating with Staff," is a good one for a small library and adds interest to a problem that is generally solved by technology.

Simple Courtesy, Empathy, and Give-and-Take

In the spirit of taking a closer look at how seemingly innocuous intentions or practices thought to be overwhelmingly positive actually need closer scrutiny, it is interesting to examine courtesy. In chapter 1, the idea of "vocational awe" was put forth by Fobazi Ettarh as something which at first seems positive (devotion to librarianship) but which can turn negative (unwavering commitment that leads to shortsightedness and burnout). In the same way, here we can examine how courtesy, civility, and give-and-take can be turned upside down when put under a microscope. While civility can be used to mask real problems and true give-and-take may not hold up in the "real" world, it is difficult to find a great deal of fault when it comes to common courtesy.

Although dysfunction and how to address personnel problems in the library were the subject of the authors' previous book, a tangential topic arose there: that of incivility. While there is great range of behaviors can be covered by the term *incivility*, in most cases it is associated with a lack of common courtesy and mutual respect. Teresa Bejan's book *Mere Civility* (2017) looks into the way the term *civility* is used and exposes some of the myths around its usefulness. She points out that civility in the past was a way to keep order in society, while currently it is a shield that people use to avoid deeper conversations. "It seems like 'civility talk' saves us the trouble of actually speaking to each other, allows us to talk past each other, signal our superior virtue, and let the audience know which side we're on," Bejan says. In this way, "civility talk" can actually deepen divisions.[5] She goes on to call for "mere civility," which confronts problems rather than putting a nice antiseptic sheen on them. "Mere civility is having the courage to make yourself disagreeable and to stay that way, but to do that while staying in the room and present to your opponents," Bejan says. "If you're talking about civility as a way to avoid an argument, as a way to isolate yourself in the more agreeable company of the like-minded who already agree with you, if you find yourself never actually speaking to anyone who fundamentally disagrees with you, you're doing civility wrong."[6] Although this deconstruction of civility seems to be at first a criticism, it is similar to the earlier discussions around empathy and diversity, where a renewed look can bring a more intentional strategy to create equality than was involved in previous efforts.

As part of a national discussion on division and divisiveness in the United States (which appeared to be peaking when *The Dysfunctional Library* came out, although it continues to the present time), the tangential topic of incivility arose. One very interesting discussion around incivility that occurred in libraries was that being nice or civil (and telling people to be so) could be seen as a form of control. Similar to the discussion in the previous chapter around empathy, perhaps not everything is quite as rosy as it seems when there is a call for civility. In fact, the idea of being "nice" has been skewered to a great degree, and there does seem to be some connection between keeping the status quo (which includes keeping marginalized people from moving forward) and remaining "civil."

Sara Ahmed, the author of *Living a Feminist Life*, has shown how complaint allows for blaming those who attempt to change the status quo. The ability to give and take may end at the "give" part. Ahmed deconstructs how complaint turns back on the complainer and instead of progressing to a place of solution, it gets bogged down in several places. In a review of a talk that she gave at the University of Birmingham, Thomas Atwater explains, "By investigating the complaint procedure itself, Ahmed hopes to recognise, firstly, how it tries to separate people and to isolate the complainer and, secondly, to emerge with new strategies for how complaint might, instead, bring people together in response to abusive structures. Her talk, then, looked also to the undermining of communal support: how complaint depletes energy, how it minimises the space that someone feels they can occupy, how its programmes of confidentiality that ostensibly protect an individual actually work to keep abuse and harassment secret and out of sight."[7] Ahmed goes on to show how those who take the time and effort to complain should at a minimum be allowed an expedited path and some understanding of their position, which is at the core of her idea of "complaint as diversity."[8]

Grappling with these commonly held beliefs surrounding behavior surely affects how individuals communicate with each other. Spending time examining how courtesy, civility, and give-and-take are viewed by deep thinkers on these subjects and in today's library can be enlightening because it can offer us ways to renew how we treat others. Within a number of these communication chapters, it can be easy to trot out standard practice and some antiquated ideas. Yet as librarians in the twenty-first century, everyone needs to be more aware and up-to-date about the thoughtful treatment of fellow employees and therefore, the community we work with every day.

Conclusion

Communication is a topic within the workplace that never seems to be fully "solved." There are continuous opportunities to use various new and improved methods to communicate. Still, regardless of one's interpersonal skills and communication style (as referenced in chapter 2), it does not matter what method one uses if one is a poor communicator. All of the chapters in this book that deal with communication propose taking the time to examine how individual libraries communicate and then implementing ways to remedy the shortcomings. Because they are a constantly moving target and there are so many communication pipelines and interactions, communication problems will always rise up. In addition to these hurdles, personnel turnover constantly introduces different personalities, and the different communication styles they bring to the job work against communication uniformity.

Despite these challenges and others, it is worth the time and effort to work towards communication improvements in your library. As library staff become more and more immersed in the information age, good communication is necessary to combat dysfunction. As indicated in the authors' article "Incivility and Dysfunction in the Library Workplace: Perceptions and Feedback from the Field" (2018) in *Library Journal*, communication disconnect is the number-one reason library workers point to when declaring their library to be dysfunctional. A functional library team by definition appears to be one that is full of workers who are well-informed and who feel strongly that they are part of a library that consistently fulfills the needs of their community (whose members, in turn, feel as though they are being listened to and spoken to). And the method by which this occurs is not nearly as important as the mutual knowledge that this connection is taking place.

QUESTIONS FOR REFLECTION

- What is the average daily amount of face-to-face interactions you have with your library colleagues? Is it too many, not enough, or a good balanced amount?

- Which communication method do you prefer in the library? Do you know which method your coworkers prefer?

- Do you think that invoking the word *empathy* can sometimes be used as a convenient excuse or as a way to avoid fully grappling with communication problems?

- What does efficient and successful communication look like in your library? What barriers are in place that don't allow your library to achieve this goal?

NOTES

1. Jade E. Davis, "Empathy and the New Mission (Decolonizing Empathy)," 2018, https://jadedid.com/blog/2018/09/27/empathy-and-the-new-mission-decolonizing -empathy/.
2. Carol Kinsey Gorman, "The Immeasurable Importance of Face-to-Face Meetings," *Forbes*, 2016, https://www.forbes.com/sites/carolkinseygoman/2016/03/11/the -immeasurable-importance-of-face-to-face-meetings/#74844aef4937.
3. Human Library Organization, "The Human Library," 2019, https://humanlibrary .org/.
4. Jo Henry, Joe Eshleman, and Richard Moniz, *The Dysfunctional Library: Challenges and Solutions to Workplace Relationships* (Chicago: American Library Association, 2018), 80–82.
5. Jill Mastrine, "Is Civility a Sham After All?" The Common Party, 2018, https://www .thecommonparty.com/single-post/2018/11/29/Is-Civility-a-Sham-After-All.
6. Mastrine, "Is Civility a Sham After All?"
7. Thomas Bridgewater, "Sara Ahmed – Mind the Gap: Complaint as Diversity Work," University of Birmingham, 2019, https://blog.bham.ac.uk/cclc/2019/02/10/sara -ahmed-mind-the-gap-complaint-as-diversity-work-30-01-2019/.
8. Sara Ahmed, "Complaint as Diversity Work," feministkilljoys, 2017, https:// feministkilljoys.com/2017/11/10/complaint-as-diversity-work/.

PART III

The Functional Leader

9

Self-Awareness
A Leader's Perspective

Self-awareness is critical for all successful employees, but most especially for leaders and managers. David Zes, reporting on an extensive study in 2013, found that leaders' self-awareness was directly linked to company performance. According to Tomas Chamorro-Premuzic, it is essential for leaders to have a high degree of self-awareness, and especially of their shortcomings.[1] Claudia Williams, likewise, believes that self-awareness is essential for building trust as a leader.[2] While not discounting accountability, the leader must also trust the staff.

Leaders face some unique challenges if they hope to become more self-aware, however. According to Tasha Eurich, "power differentials are a factor. For example, though unaware bosses have an especially detrimental impact on their employees' job satisfaction, performance, and well-being, confronting one's boss is inherently riskier because of the positional power she holds."[3] Leaders need to make a special effort to be open to feedback. As noted, it is a risky endeavor to confront one's boss or supervisor about some behavior or approach that is detrimental to the team. And if leaders are to be successful at understanding the people they lead, they must themselves possess self-awareness. According to Peter Langton, it is impossible for leaders to understand staff if they do not develop their own self-awareness first.[4]

Another important consideration is the relative effectiveness of traditional education and its ability to prepare one for a leadership role. Emotional intelligence is a key component that is often left out of higher education. In one study of effective leadership, Hougaard, Carter, and Afton note: "To be clear, we're not saying MBAs are not useful in leading an organization. But if the linear MBA-trained logic becomes the sole focus—at the cost of other skills, like self-awareness and understanding others and the culture—the leadership approach is out of balance."[5] They are not saying that there is no value in an MBA, just that it needs to be supplemented by elements such as self-awareness. And for this, some solutions should be considered.

Self-Awareness: Solutions for Leaders

Self-awareness is a critical starting point for other skill sets that a leader needs. Self-awareness alone, however, may do no good. It is worth noting that a manager who is a jerk because they knowingly rule by fear and intimidation does not necessarily lack self-awareness. They may know how they come across but just do not care to behave differently.[6] Hopefully this is rare, since most leaders have at least some desire to do good.

In arguing that managers should want to improve their self-awareness, Andy Lothian states: "What self-awareness means for managers is that they can more quickly identify competency gaps in themselves and their teams, which, in turn, promotes the skill development initiatives required to fill those gaps."[7] Lothian also makes the case that leaders should let employees know that self-knowledge is the most important kind of knowledge. It is worth unpacking this topic as solutions are considered.

A good leader should be aware of their strengths and weaknesses, so once again the importance of the self-reflective component of leadership is needed. Lothian takes this one step further. Through a combination of self-awareness and awareness of others, a leader can work to fix the shortcomings of any given team.[8] There is no doubt that this is a complex process, but a deliberate examination of strengths, weaknesses, and gaps is an excellent starting point. Magi Graziano, likewise, discusses how critical self-awareness allows leaders to address their blind spots. According to Graziano, this should lead to difficult but meaningful conversations about change.[9] This latter point is especially important. The need for change will bring to the surface a certain amount of discomfort, especially in cases where there is a mismatch between one's espoused goals or beliefs and the external perception of one's self. A true leader must be willing to wade into this discomfort.

Self-Awareness in Leadership: Examples from a First-Time Chair

MAGGIE MASON SMITH, Library Specialist,
Robert Muldrow Cooper Library, Clemson University

In September 2018 the dean of Clemson University Libraries created a Task Force to solicit online and in-person feedback from campus constituents. Despite never having participated in a Task Force such as this and having held no previous leadership role of this magnitude, I volunteered to serve as the chair of the Task Force. I learned on the go, developing my aptitude for self-awareness and refining my leadership skills based on the tasks necessary to complete the project charge. Ultimately, through the Task Force project, I was able to develop a strong foundation to continually build upon in preparation for future leadership roles.

The Task Force was working on a tight deadline; we had just over four weeks to build a blog and plan a ten-day event where volunteers manned tables across campus in order to solicit feedback. We met frequently, and I used the first meeting to gauge the communication styles and preferences of the team. I altered my own communication methods as needed: for example, I began with the idea of unplanned and organic meetings, but ultimately I started creating agendas. And although being chair meant that I needed to be somewhat involved in all aspects of the project and step in and assist if necessary, I did not micromanage. I trusted my teammates, delegating tasks according to their skill sets and interests, and I volunteered to manage tasks that were both within (writing the report) and outside (working on the blog) of my comfort zone.

Our short timeline forced us to make decisions quickly, so I had little time to second-guess my choices. I planned white space into my workday after each meeting, giving myself a dedicated time to reflect on team discussions, assess our progress, consider the changes necessary to meet our goals, and plan for those upcoming changes. I also took this time to recognize and own any mistakes—not all chosen tabling locations were ideal, for example—forgiving myself and working to resolve them if possible. I was open with the team about my lack of leadership experience and honest about what I didn't know, so I continually encouraged feedback regarding my role. I checked in with the team at the end of each meeting and spoke with members individually to remind them that constructive criticism was welcome.

Outside of the criticism requested from my teammates, I sought advice from a trusted, third-party mentor. After reflecting on a meeting, receiving feedback from a teammate, or engaging in a passionate Task Force conversation, I assessed my own actions and attitude, formed a plan, and then held a discussion with my mentor, who is familiar with my strengths and weaknesses and can provide an outsider's insight for consideration. I continued to request advice from my mentor after the Task Force ended as well, since criticism from colleagues external to the Task Force is inevitable but often hard to accept. And finally, in the time since the Task Force's end, I have sought training through self-awareness webinars, attendance at leadership-based conference presentations, and on-campus self-assessment workshops.

The Task Force gathered a total of 804 responses during the ten-day event. These responses have been and will continue to be considered when planning for the future of the Clemson Libraries. We were successful, in part, because of the working relationships on the team; those working relationships were strengthened through repeated self-assessment and conscious leadership goals. My responsibilities as Task Force chair ended in December, but self-assessment is an ongoing task. I continue to seek training and opportunities to improve my self-assessment and leadership skills in preparation for future leadership roles.

Another solution to self-awareness, and possibly the most important one, is to develop a mindful practice. According to Julie Chesley, "Change leaders with higher mindfulness are more likely to practice self-awareness and self-care as coping mechanisms for themselves when faced with ambiguity."[10] While some problems come with easy answers, most do not. It is critical for a leader to be able to wade into that ambiguity and uncertainty. Mindful practice can help in this regard. This could include breathing meditation, body scan meditation, journaling, yoga, tai chi, walking meditation, and breathing exercises. Too often, individuals get caught up in a situation and are tempted to respond reactively. But, in the words of Stephen Covey, "we have the ability to choose our response in any given set of circumstances."[11] We are so often on autopilot that we forget that between any stimulus and response there is an opportunity to choose that response. This can be especially hard for a manager or leader who likes to charge forward solving problems. Taking a step back can be helpful. Mindful practice such as meditation essentially serves as "exercise" for one's brain. This can create a metacognitive awareness that we are not our thoughts. Rather, individuals can choose which thoughts they pay attention to and act upon. This is really the highest level of internal self-awareness.

There are other strategies that can help improve self-awareness that are related to mindfulness. Jeff Gero believes that meditation helps make better leaders, since it helps deal with obstructive thoughts.[12] Dacher Keltner points out the need to reflect on and be aware of changes that individuals make and how those may affect others as well.[13]

An Author's Self-Reflection

One thing we all do way too much of is multitasking. Most studies show that we cannot really be effective while doing this. Managers and leaders who are swamped may be tempted to juggle many things at once. One thing that I have learned, however, is that when a staff member comes to me with an issue, I need to either ask them to come back at another time or stop what I am doing to listen to them. Many years ago, I started the practice of shutting my monitor off or at least minimizing everything and blocking notifications on my screen if I am engaged in an important conversation.

Hougaard et al. recommend mindfulness but also emphasize self-care (short breaks) and listening to others.[14] Listening is covered repeatedly in this book, but it is important to consider it in this context. Most people like energetic leaders. In fact, a certain positive, "can do" attitude could be considered an important leadership trait. Often individuals (not just leaders) do not listen but rather talk a lot because they are exceptionally driven and eager to implement and share their ideas. While this is not a bad thing, it does illustrate how leaders may need to be more deliberate in giving space for others. As has been shown in several studies of teaching and is stated on the TeacherVision website, "Classroom observations reveal that teachers typically wait less than 1 second for students to respond to a question."[15] One second! While challenging, a leader must be confident and self-aware enough to allow a wider space for others to interject.

Another important element of self-awareness is to recognize when one has made a mistake and apologize. David Pauleen notes that self-awareness among great leaders requires being able to *publicly* admit when they are wrong.[16] Most of us recognize that a good leader is able to admit and learn from mistakes. Everyone makes them!

Above all, leaders need to be flexible and adapt within different contexts. They also need to be able to step forward even when it may be uncomfortable to do so. Crossan and Smith report a study which exposed a number of leaders in this regard. Study participants were asked about their willingness to stand up to a bully. The experimenter then contrived a situation whereby a new employee was repeatedly bullied in front of these other leaders, and nobody spoke up or stepped in to stop the behavior.[17] Self-awareness is not just about who individuals think they are and what they think they would do. Rather, it requires them to explore the difference between their espoused values and their actual behavior. This is useful to anyone, but to leaders especially.

In a series of useful queries a leader can ask: "Do I let my experiences and biases limit how I make decisions or devalue the views of others? Do I have too much desire to control, influence, or determine the outcome? Do I focus too much on low-hanging fruit (quick wins) at the expense of making the right decision with the help and input of others? Do I allow the fear of failure to distract me from trusting others?"[18]

A last word from Eurich is equally valuable here as well: "self-awareness is not a one-and-done exercise. It is a continual process of looking inward, questioning and discovering things that have been there all along . . . the fact that we are never 'finished' becoming self-aware is also what makes the journey so exciting."[19]

Conclusion

Self-awareness is an important element in the scope of emotional intelligence. Library leaders should begin with honest self-reflection. Additionally, incorporating mindful practices improves self-awareness. Leaders should acquire the ability to publicly admit mistakes and apologize, and also be flexible and acquire a willingness to adapt to different contexts.

QUESTIONS FOR DISCUSSION

- How self-aware am I?
- Do my direct reports, peers, and supervisors see me the way I see myself?
- How can I get more feedback on how others perceive me?
- What are the things I know to be true about myself that are rooted in my core values?
- How might I work on a daily basis to become more self-aware as a leader?

NOTES

1. Tomas Chamorro-Premuzic, "How to Work for a Boss Who Lacks Self-Awareness," *Harvard Business Review* (online), April 3, 2018.
2. Claudia Williams, "Talent, IQ No Longer Enough to Lead," *Central Penn Business Journal* (May 26, 2017): 10.
3. Tasha Eurich, "Working with People Who Aren't Self-Aware," *Harvard Business Review Digital Articles* (October 19, 2018): 30.
4. Peter Langton, "The Golden Rule Is Wrong," *TD: Talent Development* 70, no. 7 (July 2016): 72–73.
5. Rasmus Hougaard, Jacqueline Carter, and Marissa Afton, "Self-Awareness Can Help Leaders More Than an MBA Can," *Harvard Business Review Digital Articles* (January 12, 2018): 2–5.
6. Eurich, "Working with People Who Aren't Self-Aware."
7. Andy Lothian, "The Dollars and Sense behind Self-Awareness," *Training* 54, no. 2 (March 2017): 16.
8. Lothian, "The Dollars and Sense behind Self-Awareness."
9. Magi Graziano, "21st-Century Leadership Intelligence: Three Tenets to Evolve as a Leader," *Leadership Excellence* 34, no. 2 (February 2017): 40–41.
10. Julie Chesley and Avonlie Wylson, "Ambiguity: The Emerging Impact of Mindfulness for Change Leaders," *Journal of Change Management* 16, no. 4 (December 2016): 329.
11. Covey as quoted by Ellen M. Heffes, "Stephen Covey on Managing Yourself and Others," *Financial Executive* 22, no. 1 (January-February 2006).
12. Jeff Gero, "Do Meditators Make Better Leaders? They Can Be Great Sources of Inspiration to Employees," *Leadership Excellence* 35, no. 1 (January 2018): 18–19.
13. Dacher Keltner, "Don't Let Power Corrupt You," *Harvard Business Review* 94, no. 10 (October 2016): 112–15.

14. Hougaard, Carter, and Afton, "Self-Awareness Can Help Leaders More Than an MBA Can," 2–5.
15. TeacherVision, "Your Secret Weapon: Wait Time," TeacherVision, https://www.teachervision.com/your-secret-weapon-wait-time.
16. David Pauleen and Ali Intezari, "Managing a Path to Wisdom," *NZ Business + Management* 31, no. 5 (June 2017): M4–5.
17. Mary Crossan and Loretta Biscaro Smith, "Taking Leadership from Good to Great," *Ivey Business Journal* (online), (November 6, 2018).
18. Chantele Dow, "It Starts by Picking up a Mirror: An Introspective Look at Inclusive Leadership," *Armed Forces Comptroller* 62, no. 4 (fall 2017): 21.
19. Tasha Eurich, *Insight: Why We're Not as Self-Aware as We Think, and How Seeing Ourselves Clearly Helps Us Succeed at Work and in Life* (New York: Crown, 2017), 258.

10

Skills Development

As in most organizations, the leadership skills needed in libraries are wide-ranging and varied. The Library Leadership & Management Association (LLAMA) points to fourteen foundational competencies in this regard, including change management, collaboration, critical thinking, project management, and marketing.[1] These areas involve both leadership qualities as well as duties performed on the job. Since this book is focused on solutions for library dysfunction, those skills and attributes which can resolve dysfunction will be the focus here. LLAMA points to the need for personnel conflict resolution skills, as well as other attributes which may correct dysfunction, such as emotional intelligence and forward thinking or vision among leaders. A study of exemplary public library leaders at all levels identified the qualities of "high emotional intelligence, characterized by empathy, the ability to control feelings and handle stress, and optimism," in addition to the ability to "promote harmonious relationships."[2] A 2013 study found that among the attributes of library administrators across all types of libraries which may aid the handling of dysfunction are empathy, vision, and good communication skills.[3]

This chapter will focus in on some of these skills which can directly heal library conflict and dysfunction, and it will expand on the importance of leader authenticity, vision, role-modeling, and learned empathy.

Authenticity

Authenticity is the display of one's true self and can lead to the well-being of employees, increased productivity, work engagement, and reduced turnover.[4] A number of researchers have defined authenticity in various ways, but it is generally understood to have both a cognitive and a behavioral dimension. The cognitive dimension includes awareness and unbiased processing, which result in "acting in concordance with one's own true self and being genuine in one's interactions and relations."[5] Barrett-Lennard defined authenticity as an interaction of three aspects—experience, awareness, and behavior.[6] Authentic individuals are aware of their experiences and how these may contrast with their personal beliefs. This evolves into actions that align with personal beliefs which may, to some extent, be influenced by others.[7] Golman and Kernis add a fourth aspect, which is applying "openness and truthfulness in one's close relationships."[8]

Leaders can find the key to authenticity in both their individual uniqueness and their sense of belonging to a work group (conforming to group norms). Followers interpret leaders as authentic when the leader is seen as unique but also has a low sense of belonging. However, leaders are also deemed authentic when they do conform to group norms but do not have any unique individual qualities. If both attributes are high or low, leaders are viewed as inauthentic. Distortion or inaccurate communications by leaders also result in inauthentic status.[9]

FIVE TRAITS OF AUTHENTIC LEADERS

1. "Pursuing their purpose with passion
2. Practicing solid values
3. Leading with their hearts as well as their heads
4. Establishing connected relationships
5. Demonstrating self-discipline"

SOURCE: Bill George, "Truly Authentic Leadership," *U.S. News & World Report*, October 30, 2006, https://www.billgeorge.org/articles/truly-authentic-leadership/.

**TIPS FOR ACHIEVI'
AUTHENTICITY IN LEA'**

- Understand personal valu⌐
- Balance extrinsic and intrinsic ⌐
- Develop a peer support group.
- Balance personal and professional lives.
- Stay grounded.
- Inspire others.

SOURCE: Michelle Brandon, "Seven Ways to Develop Your Authentic Leadership Style," *Forbes,* last updated March 13, 2018, https://www.forbes.com/sites/forbes coachescouncil/2018/03/13/seven-ways-to-develop-your -authentic-leadership-style/#f1c716e69e64.

For insight into authenticity, leaders should explore these questions: "What are my strengths? What are my weaknesses? What are the unique characteristics that I bring to the job?" For leaders striving for conformity to their organization's culture, the questions may be: "How does the organization's culture support me? What are the organizational resources I can tap into? How can I reflect the organization's mission?"

Vision and Goal Alignment

Vision has been defined as an "organizational compass" which includes organizational "goals and strategies."[10] It is a major component of an organization's identity. According to a 2013 study, 114 library leaders across all library types indicated vision as the second most important quality of an administrator.[11] More recently, a 2018 study of academic librarians found visionary thinking as the second most important trait of future library leaders.[12] While vision and goal alignment are positives for organizations, a poorly constructed or delivered vision leads to dysfunction in the ranks. Libraries are susceptible to dysfunctions stemming from vision because they are hierarchical in structure, with the vision often crafted by higher administration without input from library workers. Moreover, communicating a vision and goals may be challenging for libraries that have many divisions and branches, often in different physical locations.[13]

n correctly conveyed, vision has been shown to be inspiring to s and to reduce conflict within their library teams.[14] Studies also that a well-communicated vision can energize employees and give n a sense of purpose in their work.[15] In fact, vision has been found to a greater influence on work performance than the personality of the eader.[16] However, an organization's vision may often be viewed as something that administrators developed, and which is unrelated to the goals of employees.[17] This can make communicating the vision challenging for leaders. Maureen Orey has found the following top three vision mistakes that organizations make:

1. Failure to clearly articulate a vision.
2. Failure to communicate the vision effectively.
3. Misalignment of goals and actions to the vision.[18]

Thus, creating and conveying the library's vision to employees is a critical part of a leader's responsibility to promote a functional workplace.

In crafting the vision, leaders should base it on analyzing the organization's current state and making the vision achievable. Leaders should also connect the vision to the "values and beliefs of others," including staffers, in order to encourage commitment.[19] As stated by the ALA Office for Intellectual Freedom, this vision is linked to the mission "that defines the library's purpose and describes who the library serves."[20] As illustrated in figure 10.1, these concepts are then further broken down until they are connected to staffers' goals and actions.

FIGURE 10.1
How Vision Links to Employee Actions

Once crafted, the vision should be clearly conveyed. It is shared in writing and is repetitively reviewed with the staffers through multiple formats, verbal images, and examples.[21] A well-written vision statement is best conveyed in five minutes or less to be successful.[22] James Kouzes and Barry Posner, authors of *The Leadership Challenge*, suggest animating the vision by giving it a name or symbol or by creating an image of it and conveying it with enthusiasm.[23] If these conditions are met, the library vision will have a positive impact on the organization.

EMPLOYEE GOAL-VISION ALIGNMENT EXERCISE

1. Employees write their top 5–10 duties.

2. Managers write their view of the employees' top 5–10 duties.

3. The lists are compared and assessed for their alignment with the organization's vision.

SOURCE: Maureen Orey, "Results-Based Leadership," *Industrial and Commercial Training* 43, no. 3 (2011): 150.

Moving FOREWORD for a Trusting Workplace

LAJUAN S. PRINGLE, Branch Leader,
Charlotte Mecklenburg Library

In 2017, the Charlotte Mecklenburg Library embarked on a plan to intentionally change and strengthen its organizational culture. The library's goal was to better understand its current culture, identify the culture that would be needed to best serve the community of Mecklenburg County in the future, and create a plan of transformation. The organizational culture's focus was based on the library's strategic planning efforts, which asked: How will the library transform to meet the community's needs in 2025? The library created the Library Culture Project team to better address this question. Under the guidance of the library's CEO and its Human Resources leader, staff from across the organization were selected to participate on the team. The team utilized focus groups, surveys, conference calls and other forms of data collection to gain information regarding staff members' viewpoints of the organizational culture and what could be done to improve it. Once the collected data was analyzed, the Culture Project team went on to form the library's culture initiative, which was formally branded as *FOREWORD*. In defining *FOREWORD*, the project team issued the following statement:

Each organization, and its brand(s), has a story. And in the Charlotte Mecklenburg Library system, we are its authors. We are a trusted, collaborative and passionate group of curators, connectors and enablers. What our customers and community seek, we help find, whether that be information or resources for education, work or pleasure. We have the purpose and privilege of equalizing and improving the lives of all of our citizens and advancing our community through trusted content, knowledge and connections. We are the keepers of our history and the gateway to the future. We improve lives and connect the communities in our system, creating a contagious joy that fuels our mission. In all that we do, we help write the next chapter for Mecklenburg County so that together, we move *FOREWORD*.

Six principles were created to help define the culture of *FOREWORD* as envisioned by our staff. They are:

1. Every Voice Counts (diversity, communication, ideas appreciated)
2. We Over Me (collaboration, teamwork)
3. Think and Act Forward (change, agility, innovation)
4. Love What You Do (passion, joy)
5. Live Your Purpose (accountability, integrity, honesty)
6. Be a Hero (service, hospitality)

Once the framework for *FOREWORD* was formed, the Culture Project team was revamped to include library leaders who would lead *FOREWORD*'s implementation and engagement efforts; an implementation team to assist with carrying out recommendations formed by the Culture Project team; and "ambassadors" from each branch location. To date, the *FOREWORD* initiative has resulted in:

- Creation of a monthly e-mail newsletter that highlights a culture principle of the month, and staff activity inspired by either the highlighted principle or by others.
- Implementation of a rewards and recognition program called Shout Out! that enables staff to recognize each other for any efforts that embody the six principles of *FOREWORD*.
- The beginning of another staff rewards program where all staff are now able to borrow library materials without paying any overdue fines if they are late.

FOREWORD is a long-term initiative that the library views as an ongoing commitment to its staff. The library will periodically evaluate the initiative to address its growth as this becomes necessary. But the *FOREWORD* initiative serves as an example of what can be done to shape a workforce into a kind and caring one.

Role-Modeling

Leader role-modeling can also promote a positive and functioning library workplace. It involves the "attributes of people in social roles" which are viewed by others as similar, whereas that individual tries to be like them "by emulating those attributes."[24] It is a form of social learning. Kouzes and Posner describe leaders as "ambassadors of shared values." Leaders who are visible to their employees and deemed authentic can lead with good behavior and, by their own example, encourage such actions in those whom they oversee.[25]

In a study of 318 academic librarians, role-modeling ranked as fifth in importance, and librarians saw it as "balancing [the leader's] enthusiasm with practicality and . . . realism with optimism" and having a sense of humor.[26] Role-modeling also involves ethical leadership. Studies indicate that ethical leadership results in a more "aspirational" and "integrated" workforce and has a significant influence on employees.[27] Lastly, a 2014 study of medical library directors found that 92 percent believed that ethical leadership is based in either trust and integrity or role-modeling.[28] The actions and behavior of library leaders as positive role models can significantly impact the dynamics of the workplace.

There are a number of ways library leaders can take on the task of serving as a positive role model, including self-awareness and self-assessment. A leader must ask these questions: "Do my actions match what I tell others to do? Do I represent my team outside of my department in a positive way? Do I consistently apply standards to all of my team members? Do I personally reflect the organization's values?"[29]

Other modeling suggestions offered by Kouzes and Posner include devoting time to what is deemed important, keeping promises, and listening and adjusting to employee feedback. They also recommend repeating

---

LEADER TIPS FOR PROMOTING ROLE-MODELING

- Discuss examples of positive behavior in other workers.
- Identify role models in the organization at all levels.
- Identify the traits of good role models in the organization.
- Credit peers who exemplify positive work behaviors.
- Provide positive reinforcement to employees who reflect desired behaviors.

SOURCE: Sarah Cook and Steve Macaulay, "Making a Difference," *Training Journal*, April 2014: 35–36.

similar phrases to invoke desired feelings in the workplace, and asking how their own actions make employees feel. The use of visuals, such as positive examples, is also a method of illustration.[30] Modeling civil behaviors such as use of words, active listening, limiting negative gossip, demonstrating cooperation and teamwork, and utilizing emotional intelligence attributes is also recommended as library leaders journey towards becoming positive role models.[31]

Learned Empathy

Empathy is the ability to understand the feelings of others and what causes those feelings. Richard Boyatzis defines empathy as a social intelligence and identifies it as one of the critical leadership components involved in coaching, inspiration, influence, conflict management, and teamwork.[32] Empathy involves sensitivity and awareness and is an important part of Dan Goleman's concept of emotional intelligence. For library leaders, empathy is essential for understanding a variety of workplace dynamics such as change resistance, interpersonal relations, and even burnout. Empathy can involve *affective* empathy, which is application of the correct emotion in the situation, and *cognitive* empathy, which is the ability to understand and see things from another's perspective.[33] Steven Bell sees empathy as a way library leaders can build support and gain followers, and it is vital to overcoming change resistance.[34] For future library leaders, one study indicates empathy as the most important quality for library leaders to possess.[35]

STEPS TOWARD EMPATHIC CONVERSATIONS

- Listen to the speaker's words and tone.
- Interpret the body language of the speaker.
- Sense the true communication.
- Connect the heart to how the other person feels.
- While empathy may not come naturally to library leaders, it can be learned.

SOURCE: Joan Cheverie and Susan Gollnick, "Developing Empathy Will Make You a Better Leader," Educause, last updated March 26, 2018, https://er.educause.edu/blogs/2018/3/developing-empathy-will-make-you-a-better-leader.

Several studies found that leaders who worked to understand employees and situations better saw positive shifts in their empathy scores.[36] Empathy for others can be expressed "in terms of joy, sorrow, excitement, misery, pain, and confusion."[37] (Curious readers can try the "Empathy Quotient" test at https://psychology-tools.com/.) Elizabeth Borges suggests three steps to activating empathy: (1) identify the other person's emotion, (2) relate to that emotion, and (3) use words/actions to address the emotion positively.[38] Leaders can develop empathy by listening to employees and asking clarifying questions. Getting out of the office, walking around the library, or being a worker for a day can also bring the awareness which is critical for empathy.[39] In *Practical Empathy for Collaboration and Creativity in Your Work* (2015) by Indi Young, developing empathy involves getting "past the surface level of what people tell you."[40] This involves listening, following the topic, verifying your understanding, being sincerely supportive, showing respect, and neutralizing your personal reactions.[41] Empathy is a way of connecting with employees and understanding their everyday trials, and is a part of being an authentic leader.

Conclusion

There are many skills and qualities that library leaders can learn to minimize library dysfunction. These include being authentic and creating or conveying the library's vision with enthusiasm and creativity. Moreover, leaders have a responsibility to serve as positive role models and to show empathy for their employees.

QUESTIONS FOR DISCUSSION

- Am I an authentic leader and if so, how?
- Is the library vision communicated to and understood by library workers?
- What actions can I take to be a better role model?
- Am I truly leading with empathy? Do my direct reports feel understood and supported by me?

NOTES

1. LLAMA, "Leadership and Management Competencies—White Paper," http://www
   .ala.org/llama/sites/ala.org.llama/files/content/LLAMA%20Foundational%20
   Competencies%20-%20White%20Paper.pdf.
2. Ken Haycock, "Exemplary Public Library Branch Managers: Their Characteristics
   and Effectiveness," *Library Management* 32, no. 4/5 (2011): 270.
3. Anthony S. Chow and Melissa Rich, "The Ideal Qualities and Tasks of Library
   Leaders: Perspectives of Academic, Public, School, and Special Library
   Administrators," *Library Leadership & Management* 27, no. 1 (2013): 7.
4. Germano Reis, Jordi Trullen, and Joana Story, "Perceived Organizational Culture
   and Engagement: The Mediating Role of Authenticity," *Journal of Managerial
   Psychology* 31, no. 2 (2016): 1092, 1099.
5. Julie Menard and Luc Brunet, "Authenticity and Well-Being in the Workplace: A
   Mediation Model," *Journal of Managerial Psychology* 26, no. 4 (2011): 332.
6. Alex Matthew Wood, P. Alex Linley, John Maltby, Michael Baliousis, and Stephen
   Joseph, "The Authentic Personality: A Theoretical and Empirical Conceptualization
   and the Development of the Authenticity Scale," *Journal of Counseling Psychology* 55,
   no. 3 (2008): 386.
7. Wood, Linley, et al., "The Authentic Personality."
8. B. M. Goldman and M. H. Kernis, "The Role of Authenticity in Healthy
   Psychological Functioning and Subjective Well-Being," *Annals of the American
   Psychotherapy Association* 5, no. 6 (2002): 20.
9. Jo Henry, Joe Eshleman, and Richard Moniz, *The Dysfunctional Library: Challenges and
   Solutions to Workplace Relationships* (Chicago: American Library Association, 2018),
   103.
10. Raya Yoeli and Izhak Berkovich, "From Personal Ethos to Organizational Vision:
    Narratives of Visionary Education Leaders," *Journal of Educational Administration* 48,
    no. 4 (2010): 452.
11. Chow and Rich, "The Ideal Qualities and Tasks of Library Leaders."
12. Jason Martin, "What Do Academic Librarians Value in a Leader? Reflections on Past
    Positive Library Leaders and a Consideration of Future Library Leaders," *College &
    Research Libraries* 79, no. 6 (2018): 806.
13. Henry, Eshleman, and Moniz, *The Dysfunctional Library,* 26.
14. Olivier Doucet, Jean Poitras, and Denis Chenevert, "The Impacts of Leadership on
    Workplace Conflicts," *International Journal of Conflict Management* 20, no. 4 (2009):
    341, 350.
15. Anjanee Sethi and Bhavana Adhikari, "Impact of Communication 'Vision' on
    Organizational Communication Effectiveness," *International Journal of Marketing &
    Business Communication* 1, no. 3 (July 2012): 44.
16. Sethi and Adhikari, "Impact of Communication 'Vision,'" 45.
17. Sethi and Adhikari, "Impact of Communication 'Vision,'" 43.
18. Maureen Orey, "Results-Based Leadership," *Industrial and Commercial Training* 43, no.
    3 (2011): 147.
19. Sethi and Adhikari, "Impact of Communication 'Vision,'" 44.
20. American Library Association, Office for Intellectual Freedom, "The Library
    Mission," last updated January 2018, http://www.ala.org/tools/challengesupport/
    selectionpolicytoolkit/mission.

21. Orey, "Results-Based Leadership," 148.
22. Sethi and Adhikari, "Impact of Communication 'Vision,'" 44.
23. James Kouzes and Barry Posner, *The Leadership Challenge: How to Make Extraordinary Things Happen in Organizations*, 5th ed. (San Francisco: Jossey-Bass, 2012), 139–51.
24. Michael E. Brown and Linda K. Trevino, "Do Role Models Matter? An Investigation of Role Modeling as an Antecedent of Perceived Ethical Leadership," *Journal of Business Ethics*, no. 122 (2014): 588.
25. Kouzes and Posner, *The Leadership Challenge*, 75.
26. Martin, "What Do Academic Librarians Value in a Leader?" 814.
27. Brown and Trevino, "Do Role Models Matter?" 591.
28. Mary Joan Tooey and Gretchen N. Arnold, "The Impact of Institutional Ethics on Academic Health Sciences Library Leadership: A Survey of Academic Health Sciences Library Directors," *Journal of the Medical Library Association* 102, no. 4 (October 2014): 244, https://www.ncbi.nlm.nih.gov/pmc/articles/PMC4188051/.
29. Sarah Cook and Steve Macaulay, "Making a Difference," *Training Journal*, April 2014, 37.
30. Kouzes and Posner, *The Leadership Challenge*, 96–97.
31. Henry, Eshleman, and Moniz, *The Dysfunctional Library*.
32. Richard E. Boyatzis, "Competencies as a Behavioral Approach to Emotional Intelligence," *Journal of Management Development* 28, no. 9 (September 18, 2009): 754.
33. Stuart Duff, "Empathy in Leadership," *Training Journal*, May 2019, 10.
34. Steve Bell, "Empathy as the Leader's Path to Change | Leading from the Library," *Library Journal*, October 27, 2016, https://www.libraryjournal.com/?detailStory=empathy-as-the-leaders-path-to-change-leading-from-the-library.
35. Chow and Rich, "The Ideal Qualities and Tasks of Library Leaders," 7.
36. Duff, "Empathy in Leadership," 10.
37. F. Ioannidou and V. Konstantikaki, "Empathy and Emotional Intelligence: What Is It Really About?" *International Journal of Caring Sciences* 1, no. 3 (September-December 2008): 119.
38. Elizabeth Borges, "The Secret Weapon in Deconstructing Unconscious Bias in the Workplace," SmartBrief, September 23, 2016, https://www.smartbrief.com/original/2016/09/secret-weapon-deconstructing-unconscious-bias-workplace?utm_source=brief.
39. John Tropman and James A. Blackburn, "The Necessary Traits of Exemplary Leadership," *The Effective Executive* 21, no. 3 (2018).
40. Indi Young, *Practical Empathy for Collaboration and Creativity in Your Work* (Brooklyn, NY: Rosenfeld Media, 2015), 48.
41. Young, *Practical Empathy for Collaboration and Creativity in Your Work*, 48–49.

11

Communication and the Work Environment

I f dysfunction could be distilled down to one root cause, that cause would be poor communication. One of the more obvious results of this would be library staff who don't have a unified sense of what the library's mission and goals encompass and don't feel as though they are contributing consistently to them with their work. Another easy effect to see when communication is lacking is the loss of trust stemming from the disconnect between library leadership and library staff. When considering some of the topics that are associated with dysfunction such as bullying, lack of diversity and inclusion, and change resistance, the tenuous mappings to poor communication are more difficult to sort out, but they are still present. For example, a library leader who is firmly in favor of a more diverse staff, yet does not communicate this message and plan to the staff in order to achieve it, is little better than the leader who opposes diversity. This inability to confront a dysfunction within the library applies across the board. Shying away from a bullying employee or inaction toward conflict is a type of admission that these can occur without consequences and is a tacit signal that they are acceptable. A library with poor communication simply exacerbates these dysfunctions, since demoralized library staff do not communicate problems because they are convinced the issues will not be addressed by the administration.

The communication styles that leaders use can vary widely from one leader to another, and can also be wide-ranging for the leader herself. That is to say, a single leader can employ numerous ways to communicate. Of course, the effectiveness of the communication outweighs any consideration of the method in which one decides to communicate. In the precursor to this book, *The Dysfunctional Library: Challenges and Solutions to Workplace Relationships*, the authors found that many of the barriers to a functional library had poor communication as their foundational cause. For example, distrust of fellow employees was often rooted in an inability to communicate and understand each other. Many library employees relayed the feeling of being "out of the loop" regarding communication and of not having a good idea how their work (and work goals) connected to the greater mission of the library. A solution put forth in the earlier book was the idea that library leaders need to communicate clearly and consistently.

Clarity can be an often-overlooked aspect of communication, and this situation can be even more difficult in the library environment. In the academic library, jargon often clouds communication that could be better relayed in simpler terms. In his article "'Why Do We Have So Many Freaking Acronyms?!' Some Colleges Target Jargon in the Name of Student Success,"[1] Will Jarvis points out how students (especially first-generation students) are overwhelmed by the myriad ways in which colleges are able to avoid clear communication. Often overlooked when pointing to the poor communication a library may use with its community is that this same problem can occur internally, especially for new library employees. At the core of this latter type of communication breakdown is the inadvertent lack of understanding shown by experienced staff towards the inexperienced. This can also happen during interviews, when those who have not interviewed job applicants for quite some time misinterpret some of the behavior they see (nervousness, tiredness, or repeated answers) as negative characteristics of the applicant. A practice that can help with this problem would be empathetic exercises that give interviewers more insight into how it feels to be a job candidate, such as role-playing as a student for a day or experiencing a mock interview from the candidate's perspective.

Another unnoticed aspect with regard to communication is consistency. The dean or director in academic libraries and the director or branch leader in public libraries usually has opportunities to reach all their staff, and keeping everyone up-to-date on information that impacts the library (and the parent institution, if any) is not difficult. The practices of library leaders in this regard seem to run the gamut: some of them communicate very little, and others may just offload information through e-mail without providing any context. Of course, balancing the amount of communication can be very difficult; that is, too little communication can lead to feelings of being "out of the loop," while too much of it can lead to situations where future communications are ignored. This is why context matters, and it is good practice to reinforce whether the mission of the library is being achieved and goals are being met through one's communications. One quick note here is the idea that staff should take some time to consider their role in making sure they have updated information about their library. The employee's responsibility toward information and communication was discussed in chapter 9. The position of an internal communications manager or a library communication manager can also help with the communication flow, though it is often the case that only larger libraries are able to afford this luxury.

Library leaders should not only be available and open, they should make concerted efforts to be proactive in their day-to-day communication. This means amplifying the cliché "My door is always open" to a more proactive "I hope your door is always open, because I would like to visit you face-to-face at least once a week." A prolonged disconnect between library leaders and library staff can breed distrust and dysfunction. Even on a departmental level, it can be quite good for morale to state things positively periodically, and even daily. For example, saying "We accomplished some worthwhile goals this week and fulfilled our mission of contributing to student success" is the type of statement that is not heard often enough in many libraries.

In this chapter, striving for equal treatment and including all staff are two major goals of a good communicator in the library. Another objective is encouraging library staff in a positive way, which can lead to those staff members flourishing. Meeting all of these objectives through communication and action leads to an environment of trust which is the bedrock of a functional library.

Treat Staff Equally, Apply Policies Equally

How do library leaders enforce policies equally and treat library employees equally? This problem can sometimes be much more difficult to solve than it would seem. In fact, behind many of the technological solutions that have been advanced in this regard is the concept that computers (to be more precise, artificial intelligence) will somehow resolve this type of issue. This type of solution (and its negative aspects) will be discussed a bit later. For now, let us ponder if equal treatment of staff could be achieved, and what that would require and look like.

Treating staff equally could be used as a microcosm for treating any group or individual equally. Equality focuses in on status, rights, and opportunities. Beginning with a basic inquiry into whether the library staff have equal status, rights, and opportunities leads to some structural problems. First, there are the hierarchical levels in a library organization that promote inequalities. Equal rights get addressed by library associations, but they may not be truly enforced, and opportunities seem to be available primarily to one select group, that is, the white staff who account for 77 percent of all librarians. Therefore, libraries appear to be pretty far behind when it comes to the issue of treating staff equally.

There are numerous cases made throughout this book for pathways to begin to create a world that is more equal. Obviously, libraries as institutions with a heavily skewed white workforce have a great deal of work to do. As with many problems, education about the topic leads to awareness, so a good start would be to read some of the pointers in the guide entitled "Disrupting Whiteness in Libraries and Librarianship: A Reading List"[2] developed by Karla J. Strand, the gender and women's studies librarian at the University of Wisconsin System. Library workers who do not make at least a small effort to educate themselves on these (and other social justice) issues are turning their backs on portions of the communities they serve and often their fellow library staff as well. Obviously, there are many more avenues to explore on this topic, such as those examined in "White Librarianship in Blackface: Diversity Initiatives in LIS"[3] by April Hathcock, "The Low Morale Experience of Academic Librarians" by Kaetrena Davis Kendrick, and *Topographies of Whiteness: Mapping Whiteness in Library and Information Science*,[4] edited by Gina Schlesselman-Tarango.

As shown in the book *Algorithms of Oppression: How Search Engines Reinforce Racism*[5] (2018) by Safiya Umoja Noble, computer programs that seem to assess fairly are often created with their own set of programmer biases, and those who design them can replicate their own unconscious preferences and prejudices in those systems. Noble gives many examples of how search engine results "misrepresent a variety of people, concepts, types of information and knowledge."[6] One way forward is less reliance on the internet as our sole source of information. As Barbara Fister states in her review of the book, "Noble unpacks the trouble with corporations that have no public accountability except to shareholders dominating our information landscape and, in particular, how problematic their systems are for women and people of color. The design of our most dominant information gateway poaches unpaid labor, imagines the world to be just like those who write the code to sell attention and ads, and gives us back a reflection of ourselves that is warped by jumbling information together without context."[7] Finally, Noble reminds us of the importance of libraries to everyone when she states that reliance on poorly constructed, algorithmically produced results "is further compounded by a dependence upon the Internet to supplement what society is not providing, like high-quality education, and access to libraries and other traditional sources of knowledge."[8]

Lest the librarian breathe a sigh of relief that these issues are outside the library, Matthew Reidsma in *Masked by Trust: Bias in Library Discovery* (2019) focuses a similar lens on library discovery systems. He has found that "library discovery systems struggle with accuracy, relevance, and human biases, and these shortcomings have the potential to shape the academic research and worldviews of the students and faculty who rely on them. While human bias, commercial interests, and problematic metadata have long affected researchers' access to information, algorithms in library discovery systems increase the scale of the negative effects on users, while libraries continue to promote their 'objective' and 'neutral' search tools."[9]

In Sophia Arakelyan's article "Artificial Intelligence May Reflect the Unfair World We Live in," a solution is suggested for poorly designed AI systems: "So, our dilemma is whether to 'adjust' neural networks to make them more fair in an unfair world, or address the prime causes of bias and prejudice in real life and give more opportunities to women and minorities. In this way one would (hopefully) see data naturally improve, to reflect those positive trends over time. A truly progressive society should opt for the second option."[10] Of course, this type of thinking counterposes the unquestioning drive to have these AI systems in the first place, regardless of their defects, with the belief that we should strive for a truly progressive society on its own terms, which would eventually be reflected in our AI systems.

Whether it is a person today or a machine in the future making the decisions, libraries will still need to be concerned about equality. Having failed to fully adhere to ideals such as equal access to information for all and having seemingly lost the battle for privacy (as far as the internet is concerned), libraries can still hopefully move forward with the idea that their workers are treated as fairly as possible, as difficult as this may be.

LEADERSHIP TIPS FOR CREATING A POSITIVE WORKPLACE

- Ask opinions and listen to employees.
- Get to know employees and their motivations.
- Be transparent and convey library goals clearly.
- Consistently ask employees how to improve the library.
- Recognize employees' work regularly.

SOURCE: Bill Sims, Jr., "Listen Up Bosses," *USA Today Magazine* 143, no. 2832 (September 2014): 39, http://search.ebscohost.com/login.aspx?direct=true&db=aph&AN=98390834&site=ehost-live&scope=site.

Encourage Staff to Thrive

Related to the section on the humanness inherent in libraries, especially the reference to underfunding and shrinking budgets, we come to the question of how library leaders can both motivate staff and meet an even more worthy goal: encouraging staff to thrive. Exploring what a thriving staff looks like may be a good place to begin with on this topic. In similar fashion to a number of questions about building a better workplace, leaders and staff may have dissimilar ideas on this vision. For example, some library staff may see a clean and healthy work environment as a priority, and may not place efficiency and completed workload as high in their scale as their library leader does. But there doesn't need to be a false binary constructed here, and some level of agreement can occur on a number of parameters about the workplace.

Often, thriving staff are those who feel they have opportunities to grow and develop, especially in these times of rapid change. It may be more important for the library leader to offer employees these opportunities, encourage them to grasp them, and then see how staff react. A wonderful aspect of library groups and associations is that they offer a great deal of training, webinars, events, and other avenues for professional development. Apart from these offerings, in the academic library, staff can improve their expertise through working with and learning about other campus departments and by deepening their understanding of the student experience. Students often ask questions in the library about "non-library" topics such as registration, financial aid, and the curriculum, and there are perennial inquiries about directions. This can also be the case for public librarians, who can get to know their community better by offering useful information guidance on employment resources and technical help from start to finish. Viewing the users' experience through their eyes and becoming an expert on the multifaceted needs of customers can create a very rewarding and positive workplace for all.

Establish an Environment of Trust

The concept of trusting someone is built on a mutual understanding that the person you trust will not harm you in some way. Dependent on this notion is how the relationship is designed to deal with difficulties that may spiral out of control in cases where harm is done. Libraries, despite some of the ideals placed upon them, are ultimately workplaces like any other. As Fobazi Ettarh has shown us, libraries (and their workers) cannot hide behind aspects of vocational awe when their negative traits are exposed.[11] Harm has been done by libraries, and attempting to balance that with good actions does not make the effects of that harm disappear. All of this is said to establish the idea that recognizing that harm is done points directly to environments of mistrust so this step must first be broached before establishing an environment of trust. To sum up, often library leaders may go in attempting to build an environment of trust and not recognize the environment of distrust that is already there.

Trust can center around numerous aspects. In an environment of trust, built on mutual respect and a strong support system, communication can often flow quite freely. As mentioned in chapter 13, staff bonding and team building outside regular work duties can contribute to an environment of trust. This way of establishing trust may not work in all libraries and it is stressed several times that this should not be a forced situation. However, the common idea that it is much more difficult to bring harm to someone you see as a multi-dimensional person rather than "just a number" applies here. The first step to a trustful work environment may be to be the trustful person one wants others to be (with apologies to Gandhi). Trust gets built where transparency and openness build foundations. As in many of the communication hurdles and ideals listed in this chapter, modeling the desired behavior along with being the first to trust others can serve as good ways to establish trust.

Conclusion

The communication responsibilities of leaders are much greater than those of anyone else in the library. It can be a great demonstration of mutual respect when a library leader is transparent and open to the staff she leads. Although it can be quite difficult to deliver bad news, most people feel as though they have been treated well when they are given the opportunity to hear information that may not be favorable rather than being kept in the dark.

This chapter is one of the few in the book that does not have an associated library vignette that provides a solution to one of the topics discussed. This is because an example here might allow a leader to shirk some of her responsibility as a communicator. After all, pointing out how an example may not apply or nodding in agreement while saying "I do that" lets a leader off the hook when confronting any communication problem she may have. All of the subtopics in this chapter come down to library leaders communicating to their staff the type of library they want to build. Is it a dysfunctional library that builds distrust through inequality? Is it a library that allows some to thrive while others are left out? Is a lack of communication creating or contributing to a negative workplace? Do weeks go by without a leader even saying hello to all of the employees who are looking to her for guidance as their leader? It is obvious that at the heart of any change is the work needed to improve the situation, so library leaders who are not communicating well with their library staff need to get to work.

QUESTIONS FOR REFLECTION

- Is it possible to truly treat employees fairly?
- What are some elements of the most positive workplace you have ever worked in? Can those aspects be fostered in your library?
- As a library leader, what do you do to develop trust?
- Are you aware of a library that could supply a vignette for this chapter that would provide an example of an inclusive workplace? How did they achieve this?

NOTES

1. Will Jarvis, "'Why Do We Have So Many Freaking Acronyms?!' Some Colleges Target Jargon in the Name of Student Success," *Chronicle of Higher Education*, 2019, https://www.chronicle.com/article/Why-Do-We-Have-So-Many/246839.
2. Karla J. Strand, "Disrupting Whiteness in Libraries and Librarianship: A Reading List," University of Wisconsin-Madison Libraries, 2019, https://www.library.wisc.edu/gwslibrarian/bibliographies/disrupting-whiteness-in-libraries/.

3. April Hathcock, "White Librarianship in Blackface: Diversity Initiatives in LIS," *In the Library with the Lead Pipe*, 2015, http://www.inthelibrarywiththeleadpipe.org/2015/lis-diversity/.

4. Gina Schlesselman-Tarango, ed., *Topographies of Whiteness: Mapping Whiteness in Library and Information Science* (Litwin Books & Library Juice Press, 2017), https://litwinbooks.com/books/topographies-of-whiteness/.

5. Safiya Umoja Noble, ed., *Algorithms of Oppression: How Search Engines Reinforce Racism* (New York: New York University Press, 2018), https://nyupress.org/9781479837243/algorithms-of-oppression/.

6. USC Annenberg School of Journalism and Communication, "In 'Algorithms of Oppression,' Safiya Noble Finds Old Stereotypes Persist in New Media," 2018, https://annenberg.usc.edu/news/diversity-and-inclusion/algorithms-oppression-safiya-noble-finds-old-stereotypes-persist-new.

7. Barbara Fister, "Catching Up with Safiya Noble's Algorithms of Oppression," *Library Babel Fish*, 2018, Inside Higher Ed, https://www.insidehighered.com/blogs/library-babel-fish/catching-safiya-noble%E2%80%99s-algorithms-oppression-1.

8. USC Annenberg School of Journalism and Communication, "In 'Algorithms of Oppression.'"

9. Matthew Reidsma, "New Book: *Masked by Trust: Bias in Library Discovery*," 2019, https://matthew.reidsrow.com/.

10. Sophia Arakelyan, "Artificial Intelligence May Reflect the Unfair World We Live in," *Entrepreneur*, 2017, https://www.entrepreneur.com/article/304467.

11. Fobazi Ettarh, "Vocational Awe and Librarianship: The Lies We Tell Ourselves," 2018, *In the Library with the Lead Pipe*, http://www.inthelibrarywiththeleadpipe.org/2018/vocational-awe/.

12

Conflict Management

One challenging component of the job for library leaders and managers is conflict management. Managers can spend up to 25 percent of their workweek managing conflict.[1] Aside from workload, interpersonal conflict with colleagues ranks as the biggest challenge faced by library staff.[2] Conflict management is critical to maintaining a functional workplace because conflict contributes to increased worker stress, numerous health issues, and burnout, which in turn result in higher rates of sick leave and turnover.[3] And because conflicts can escalate and often become toxic, such as in bullying or mobbing situations, the importance of manager intervention cannot be overestimated. Often, with early intervention by a leader, conflicts can be resolved with only minimal negative impact on the workplace.

Before discussing the management of negative conflict in the workplace, it should be noted that research varies regarding the impact of conflict as it relates to *tasks*, and numerous studies indicate that some types of task workplace conflict are even positive. Team performance can improve when conflict among its members is "mild in nature and prompts information gathering."[4]

Task conflict may broaden the variety of ideas and approaches and foster mutual respect for coworkers through frank discussions. De Wit, Greer, and Jehn's meta-analysis of over eighty studies indicated a positive association of task conflict with group performance, most typically in management teams with specific performance measurements and when the relationship conflict was weak.[5] Other studies also support a positive impact when task-driven group conflict is managed correctly.[6]

While there may be some positive impact resulting from conflict with regard to completing tasks, research points to the opposite result with *relationship conflict*. Relationship conflicts, such as personality differences, result in "turnover, absenteeism, and work dissatisfaction," as well as reduced productivity.[7] In her research focused on academic librarians, Kaetrena Davis Kendrick concludes that relationship conflicts are directly linked to low morale in the workplace. Among the causes of low morale are "relationship[s] that developed in a negative and unexpected manner" and "incompatible individual work relationships."[8] It is relationship conflicts which are the focus of this chapter, and which will be explored further.

Any number of causes can trigger relationship conflict. In addition to poor communication explored earlier, conflict may also arise over obtaining and using resources. Also, divisions within the library can clash if they are pursuing dissimilar goals.[9] For example, if the IT department applies filters to the computers for cybersecurity, but in doing so limits library customers' access to necessary sites, this may trigger a conflict. Relationship conflict may also arise if team members fail to pull their weight or accomplish the tasks that are necessary for group success. This type of behavior can reflect counterproductive work behavior or even bullying. Finally, there may be disagreement by staff in the areas of values, perception, and attitudes.[10] For example, one librarian may place more value on providing one-on-one instruction than on delivering group programs which increase the library's impact numbers.

Increased Self-Awareness

Like everyone, leaders face challenges with their personal tendencies, as explored in chapter 1. But they also should explore additional areas of self-awareness which research indicates can affect their management of conflict. These areas include conflict orientation, cognitive flexibility, emotion regulation, and emotional intelligence.

Conflict orientation is defined as the set of individual beliefs, tendencies, and actions which affect how a leader handles conflict in the workplace. It is the "complex of cognitive, motivational, moral, and action orientations to conflict situations that guide one's conflict behaviors and responses."[11] The first component of conflict orientation is based in personal beliefs. As adults, everyone has a series of beliefs from their upbringing and personal experiences which impact how they handle disputes and disagreements. Second, these personal beliefs and social values can impact resource distribution, which is often a source of workplace conflict. Third, the management of personal anxiety (discussed later in this chapter) also influences leaders' reactions when involved in managing conflict. Lastly, their "moral scope," or how they view others through a moral lens, can influence leaders' actions.[12] While all these areas impact leaders' actions and decisions, they also can be modified through education and self-awareness training, as explored in chapter 18.

Cognitive flexibility involves the ability of a leader to have a clear vision of both the organization as well as individuals as this relates to a given conflict. This involves understanding the interests and motivations of both parties and "see[ing] the conflict issues from other vantage points."[13] The ability to maintain this larger perspective is so important that research indicates it has more of an impact than empathy. Numerous studies find reduced aggression and retaliation and better resolutions when conflict is managed by individuals who possess cognitive flexibility.[14] Thus, a leader's ability to mentally step away from the situation and view events more broadly and objectively is more likely to produce positive conflict resolution.

Another area for leader awareness is emotion regulation, or "the ability to inhibit impulsive, automatic or . . . [highly] emotional responses to conflict."[15] These emotions can be controlled by a variety of methods such as redirecting attention, modifying the emotion through reevaluation of it, or suppressing the emotion. Redirecting attention from the emotional trigger and mentally focusing on an unemotional task can reduce the negative impact of the emotion.[16] An example of this would be mentally calculating a difficult math problem in order to reduce an emotional reaction and engage the prefrontal cortex of the brain. Studies also indicate that reevaluation of the emotional trigger—that is, recognizing the emotion and reevaluating its cause—is another successful method, especially when done earlier rather than later in the response process.[17] Finally, while suppressing the emotion is an option and will help in the short term, it can have a long-term negative mental and emotional impact on the individual if it is always the regulation method of choice.

Lastly, emotional intelligence (EI), the understanding of the emotions of one's self and others, has shown to be an indicator of successful managers. Schlaerth, Ensari, and Christian's meta-analytical review of twenty-nine studies determined that high EI led to the constructive resolution of workplace conflict.[18] High-EI leaders will be able to handle conflicts better and engage in the collaborative or cooperative approaches to conflict resolution which, as discussed later in this chapter, are often the best methods of resolving conflict.[19]

Cultural Awareness

Cultural awareness or cultural intelligence is another dimension that library leaders should be aware of, especially those who have a diverse workforce. Often leaders find themselves in situations where workers' differing culture and beliefs play a role in conflict in the library workplace. And because many libraries are increasingly diverse in their staffing, culture is playing a greater role in the workplace's dynamics. While this section will not give an extensive overview of this topic, it will review the basics of cultural dynamics and conflict which are important for library leaders to know.

Cultures can be broken down into three categories—dignity, honor, and face. Workers from dignity cultures (e.g. North America including Asian-Americans and Northern Anglos) behave according to the internal standards that they believe are right.[20] Honor culture workers (e.g. Western Egypt, Turkey, Spain, Greece, India, Southern Anglos (Latinos)) also value their own work, but this value also depends on the honor accorded to it by others.[21] This acknowledgment is essential for honor workers. Lastly, cultures of face (e.g., China, Arab, Korea, India, Japan) are based on what others think and also on hierarchy, and the worker's rank determines his level of respectability.[22]

Within the dynamics of these three types of cultures, workplace conflict can occur when belief systems clash. Dignity cultures expect "positive reciprocity," and actions are driven by what the worker believes is right. Conflict is typically handled directly by dignity cultures and instigators are confronted directly with their problematic behavior.[23] Honor culture workers must be respected and will not tolerate any "wrongs done to him or her."[24] While positive reciprocity is also a part of the honor culture, so is negative reciprocity (i.e., a payback for doing a wrong), since this is linked to the honor component of the belief system. Thus, honor culture workers can confront instigators aggressively and often with anger.[25] Face cultures expect people to work together in a formal and polite way with conflict avoided at all costs. Conflict disrupts the "harmony" of the group and the group, rather than the individual target, will retaliate against the instigator through shaming.[26]

In addressing conflict in these culturally triggered conflict situations, there are some basic guidelines. First, early intervention by the leader to prevent escalation of the conflict is important. Second, often cultural explanations of differences can be used to help facilitate resolution. Bringing the parties together and simply discussing their different belief systems may resolve the issue. Third, when cultural explanations do not work, restructuring (creating subgroups or new partnerships) should be implemented. Finally, if all else has failed, as a last resort the manager should assume a forceful or dominating stance in order to push the work group through their assigned task.[27]

Managing Conflict

It is well established that there are five conflict management styles—integrating, obliging (accommodating), dominating (competing), avoiding, and compromising. Evidence indicates that shifting through several styles, even if dealing with one particular conflict, is an effective strategy.[28] However, as leaders tend to remain in their preferred mode of conflict resolution, changing these modes may be challenging. While accommodating and collaborating are the most successful styles, avoidance is common with library leaders and often contributes to library dysfunction.[29] Similarly, in an international study of thirty libraries in management colleges, avoidance was the top-ranking conflict resolution strategy used with library workers (followed by compromising and dominating).[30]

When addressing a conflict situation between staff members, leaders should move through basic steps. First is active listening, discussion, and trying to understand the issue. This is followed by a challenging step—a discussion held either with an individual employee or as a mediator if the conflict is between two coworkers. The leader must be neutral and impartial because if the workers perceive any type of bias or favor on her part, credibility is lost, as is the ability to resolve the conflict.[31] As Peter Bell notes, "Compared to other leadership skills, be it planning or presence,

LEADER AWARENESS AND CONFLICT MANAGEMENT STYLES

High Self-Interest + Low Other Interest = Forcing Approach	High Self-Interest + High Other Interest = Collaborative Approach
Low Self-Interest + High Other Interest = Compromising/ Accommodative Approach	Low Self-Interest + Low Other Interest = Avoidance Approach

SOURCE: Debra Gilin Oore, Michael P. Leiter, and Diane E. LeBlanc, "Individual and Organizational Factors Promoting Successful Reponses to Workplace Conflict," *Canadian Psychology* 56, no. 3 (2015): 303.

difficult conversation stands out as hard to master owing to the shifting and unpredictable nature of the situations and interactions."[32] Soehner and Darling have written an excellent book, *Effective Difficult Conversations: A Step-by-Step Guide* (2016), to help library leaders in this area. The leader must also maintain "optimal ratios of positive-to-negative emotions" expressed during the conflict resolution process, and the ideal number is three positive emotions to one negative.[33] Lastly, the leader will move toward a resolution with concern, interest, and real conviction. In this step, the leader must learn to balance tension (both mental and emotional) and promote agreement between the parties.[34]

Addressing Staff Behavior

When the conversation is between a leader and an individual staff member, Maggie Farrell outlines a series of important steps to take to address staff behavior. The first element is to make sure the focus is on a specific behavior and not on someone's personality. Aside from the fact that it is difficult (or impossible) for anyone to change their personality, the reality is that personal variety and diversity in the workplace are something that managers should take efforts to protect, not squash. Adequate preparation and a focus on a limited number of issues are also important when addressing a staffer's problematic behavior.[35] This can involve practice or mentally walking through what the goal of the conversation should be. One should prepare for the possibility that the staff member may become emotional or upset. This is to be accepted, and one should not try to discount or deny those emotions the other person is experiencing. According to Nick Gold, "it is vital that they let it all out, because then you can begin to move forward."[36] Your acknowledgment of the context can also be important. It is fine to give credence to a situation being difficult when, in fact, it is. Setting can also be important, and these conversations should take place in a private or semiprivate location. Most important of all is, again, to listen. A successful outcome can best be achieved when the other person in the conversation has a chance to share their thoughts and concerns.

In considering the importance of critical conversations for the success of leaders in particular, Soehner and Darling aptly state: "The difference between a minimally successful manager and a truly successful one is the capacity for having effective difficult conversations. You will be remembered and promoted not because you manage your budget well and meet deadlines, although these are very important, but because you help the people around you reach—and maybe exceed—their professional potential. Having these conversations may never be easy, but if you follow key steps and develop needed communication skills, you will become confident in your abilities and feel satisfied that there is integrity in the way that you interact with those under your supervision."[37]

Working with some staff who are set in their ways can be challenging. Behaviors that have existed for an extended period of time will be very difficult to change and require at least some change commitment from the staff member.

TIPS FOR DELIVERING FEEDBACK TO STAFF

- Deliver information in person.
- Focus on specifics of behavior.
- Be compassionate and patient.
- Revisit issues multiple times (if needed).

SOURCE: Tasha Eurich, "Working with People Who Aren't Self-Aware," *Harvard Business Review Digital Articles* (October 19, 2018).

From Stress to Success

ANONYMOUS

When I worked at a large, urban library, I supervised staff members who worked exceedingly stressful jobs. Whereas most library employees worked a service desk 4–5 hours a day, a small group of employees at my library worked the support desk 8 hours a day. These employees were always on, and rarely had a break from helping the public. As you may know, working with the public can be exceedingly stressful. One of these employees, Nadine, began having fits of temper. Her temper would flare up when interacting with patrons, and eventually with her colleagues. The situation became so bad that she lost her cool with me and spoke to me in a way that was grounds for immediate termination. I took her back to my office and told her that "right now I am within my rights to fire you, on the spot." However, I went on, I was not going to terminate her, but give her a chance to get some help, and fix the situation. The strategy worked. She went for mental health counseling to help her deal with the stressors in her life, and ended up being one of the department's star employees.

Resolution Styles

Equally important in conflict resolution is the need for using the appropriate resolution style. One of these methods is logrolling, which is when one party relinquishes something less important in order to give the other party something of importance to them. This type of trade-off can result in a win-win scenario.[38] Resolution can also be reached by both parties exploring and agreeing on a new direction. In fact, discussions focused on mutual inquiry and idea creation rather than on politicking for one's side are more likely to be successful.[39]

Another negotiation style that leaders may use is to force or insist that their view of the resolution be enacted. There are times when force is useful, such as in an emergency situation where swift action is necessary, or as a last resort in resolving culture-based issues. However, research indicates that

---

IS COACHING FOR YOU?

- Is Coaching for You?
- Are you capable of managing personal conflicts and being a role model?
- Do you have the skill set to coach?
- Does coaching involve a personal conflict with the staffer?

SOURCE: Daniel B. Griffith, "The Leader's Role in Coaching Employees through Conflict," HigherEdJobs, last updated April 18, 2016, https://www.higheredjobs .com/articles/articleDisplay.cfm?ID=882.

the use of force "often has little lasting effect and can also bring about unintended consequences that only perpetuate the problems."[40] Instead, leaders should try to understand the root cause of the conflict, and work towards resolving that issue.

While time-consuming, coaching is a positive approach to conflict. When leaders act as coaches, they spend time exploring the facts and talking with the impacted workers. One aspect of coaching that is critical for leaders is to understand what their own personal style of conflict resolution is. The leaders must be aware of their own tendencies—competing, collaborating, compromising, avoiding, or accommodating—if using the coaching model. (A simple way to analyze your personal conflict style, "Self-Assessment: Conflict Management Style Orientation Scale," can be found in Steven L. McShane's book *Canadian Organizational Behaviour,* and online at https://mheducation.ca/college/mcshane4/student/olc/4obm_sa_13.html.) When coaching an employee, leaders should explore compromising and collaborative outcomes, new approaches and strategies for personal interactions, and reframing the disagreement in terms of a win-win outcome.[41] Finally, coaching can also take the role of retraining employees' actions or approaches in order to reduce incidents of workplace conflict.

CONFLICT MANAGEMENT TIPS

- Rotate staff members to a new work group/department.
- Create opportunities for staff to bond through social events.
- Reiterate the greater, common goal of the organization or department.
- Provide a manual for operations and methods.
- Allow for flexibility in rules or procedures when appropriate.

SOURCE: Shenu Aliyu Mukhtar, "Organizational Conflict Management Strategies on Employee Job Satisfaction: A Conceptual Relationship," *International Journal of Medical Research and Review* 3, no. 5 (May 2013): 2859.

Conclusion

Conflict resolution can be challenging for library leaders. Understanding this role begins with an awareness of one's own preferred conflict management styles, emotional regulation, and emotional intelligence. In diverse workplaces, cultural intelligence is also important. Also important is the ability to feel comfortable with various methods of conflict management and flexibility, since use of the appropriate method for the situation offers a better chance for resolving issues. Throughout the process, leaders should attempt to remain neutral, emphasize positive over negative emotions, and try to relieve tension between the parties during the resolution process.

QUESTIONS FOR REFLECTION

- Do I have personal beliefs that may impact my ability to resolve conflict?
- What is my preferred conflict resolution style?
- Am I able to regulate my emotions during conflict resolution?
- Can I switch resolution styles to fit the situation?
- Are there any conflicts or potential conflicts related to culture in my workplace?

NOTES

1. Dartmouth College, Trustees of Dartmouth College, "Faculty/Employee Assistance Program: Resolving Workplace Conflict," https://www.dartmouth.edu/~eap/search -results.html?q=conflict&sa=search.
2. Jo Henry, Joe Eshleman, and Richard Moniz, *The Dysfunctional Library: Challenges and Solutions to Workplace Relationships* (Chicago: American Library Association, 2018).
3. Debra Gilin Oore, Michael P. Leiter, and Diane E. LeBlanc, "Individual and Organizational Factors Promoting Successful Reponses to Workplace Conflict," *Canadian Psychology* 56, no. 3 (2015): 301.
4. Oore, Leiter, and LeBlanc, "Individual and Organizational Factors," 301.
5. Frank R. C. de Wit, Linred L. Greer, and Karen A. Jehn, "The Paradox of Intragroup Conflict: A Meta-Analysis," *Journal of Applied Psychology* 97, no. 2 (2012): 360–90, http://dx.doi.org/10.1037/a0024844.
6. Leslie Dechurch and Michelle A. Marks, "Maximizing the Benefits of Task Management: The Role of Conflict Management," *International Journal of Conflict Management* 12, no. 1 (2001).
7. Oore, Leiter, and LeBlanc, "Individual and Organizational Factors," 301.
8. Kaetrena Davis Kendrick, "The Low-Morale Experience of Academic Librarians: A Phenomenological Study, *Journal of Library Administration* 57, no. 8 (2017): 851, 853.
9. David Payne, "Harnessing Conflict," *Library Leadership and Management* 24, no. 1 (winter 2010): 8.
10. Shenu Aliyu Mukhtar, "Organizational Conflict Management Strategies on Employee Job Satisfaction: A Conceptual Relationship," *International Journal of Medical Research and Review* 3, no. 5 (May 2013): 2858.

11. Peter T. Coleman, "Wisdom: Meta-Competencies for Engaging Conflict in a Complex, Dynamic World," *Negotiation Journal* 34, no. 1 (January 2018): 15.

12. Coleman, "Wisdom: Meta-Competencies for Engaging Conflict," 15.

13. Oore, Leiter, and LeBlanc, "Individual and Organizational Factors," 303.

14. Oore, Leiter, and LeBlanc, "Individual and Organizational Factors," 303

15. Coleman, "Wisdom: Meta-Competencies for Engaging Conflict," 16.

16. Jamie Ferri and Greg Hajcak, "Neural Mechanisms Associated with Reappraisal and Attentional Deployment," *Current Opinion in Psychology* 3 (June 2015): 17–21, https://www.ncbi.nlm.nih.gov/pmc/articles/PMC4331032/.

17. Yan Hunping, Na Lin, Lixia Cui, and Qin Zhang, "Is Reappraisal Always Effective in Modifying Emotional Reactions in Females? The Role of Regulatory Timing and Goals," *Brain Behavior* 8, no. 2 (February 2018), https://www.ncbi.nlm.nih.gov/pmc/articles/PMC5822571/.

18. Andrea Schlaerth, Nurcan Ensari, and Julie Christian, "A Meta-Analytical Review of the Relationship between Emotional Intelligence and Leaders' Constructive Conflict Management," *Group Processes & Intergroup Relations* 16, no. 1 (2013): 130–33.

19. Margaret M. Hopkins and Robert D. Yonker, "Managing Conflict with Emotional Intelligence: Abilities That Make a Difference," *Journal of Management Development* 34, no. 2 (2005): 229.

20. Angela K.-Y. Lueng and Dov Cohen, "Within- and Between-Culture Variation: Individual Differences and the Cultural Logics of Honor, Face, and Dignity Cultures," *Journal of Personality and Social Psychology* 100, no. 3 (March 2011): 508.

21. Lueng and Cohen, "Within- and Between-Culture Variation," 508.

22. Lueng and Cohen, "Within- and Between-Culture Variation," 509.

23. Jeanne Brett, "Intercultural Challenges in Managing Workplace Conflict—A Call for Research," *Cross Cultural & Strategic Management* 25, no. 1 (2018): 39.

24. Lueng and Cohen, "Within- and Between-Culture Variation," 508.

25. Brett, "Intercultural Challenges in Managing Workplace Conflict," 38.

26. Lueng and Cohen, "Within- and Between-Culture Variation," 508.

27. Brett, "Intercultural Challenges in Managing Workplace Conflict," 47–48.

28. Oore, Leiter, and LeBlanc, "Individual and Organizational Factors," 304.

29. Jo Henry, Joe Eshleman, Rebecca Croxton, and Richard Moniz, "Incivility and Dysfunction in the Library Workplace: Perceptions and Feedback from the Field," *Journal of Library Administration* 58, no. 2 (2018).

30. Vijayakumar Mallappa and Manoj Kumar K.S., "Conflict Management in Management Library Professionals," *Journal of Library & Information Technology* 35, no. 3 (May 2015): 204.

31. Ravinder Jit, Chandra Shekhar Sharma, and Mona Kawatra, "Servant Leadership and Conflict Resolution: A Qualitative Study," *International Journal of Conflict Management* 27, no. 4 (2016): 603.

32. Steven Bell, "Leading a Difficult Conversation: There Is Help | Leading from the Library," *Library Journal,* April 27, 2017, https://www.libraryjournal.com/?detailStory=leading-a-difficult-conversation-there-is-help-leading-from-the-library.

33. Coleman, "Wisdom: Meta-Competencies for Engaging Conflict," 17.

34. Coleman, "Wisdom: Meta-Competencies for Engaging Conflict," 17.

35. Maggie Farrell, "Difficult Conversations," *Journal of Library Administration* 55, no. 4 (2015): 303.

36. Nick Gold, "How to Conduct Difficult Conversations," *People Management* (August 2017): 44.

37. Catherine Soehner and Ann Darling, "We've All Been There: Conducting Effective Difficult Conversations," *American Libraries* 49, no. 3/4 (March 2018): 42–45.

38. Elizabeth Ruth Wilson and Leigh L. Thompson, "Creativity and Negotiation Research: The Integrative Potential," *International Journal of Conflict Management* 25, no. 4 (2014): 305.

39. Coleman, "Wisdom: Meta-Competencies for Engaging Conflict," 18.

40. Coleman, "Wisdom: Meta-Competencies for Engaging Conflict," 20–21.

41. Daniel B. Griffith, "The Leader's Role in Coaching Employees through Conflict," HigherEdJobs, last updated April 18, 2016, https://www.higheredjobs.com/articles/articleDisplay.cfm?ID=882.

13

Facilitate Collaboration

Making an action or process easy or easier would at first glance appear to be quite beneficial. One could state that our current time is an age of efficiency, where the common goal is to have a library staff who work in a well-organized and competent way. In many libraries, one common desire is to emulate how businesses function and thereby achieve a well-facilitated organization. The need for efficiencies and well-run organizations drives how many library leaders see their value. What, then, does all of this talk about efficiency mean to a library leader who is facilitating collaboration inside and outside of her library? Related to this topic is reevaluating the narratives around effectiveness and productivity and examining the human effects associated with them.

General terminology can often abdicate responsibility and lead to a great deal of dysfunction. In other words, a leader needs to be very specific and focused when discussing how things are to be done. Lip service to diversity and inclusion has already been discussed in previous chapters. Platitudes and vague allusions to collaboration are often seen through by the staff, and unfulfilled idealism can foster cynicism. A library leader who can facilitate true collaboration will take some time to analyze the current situation in her library, in a way akin to the communication environment evaluations discussed in earlier chapters. Attentively taking this information and creating a collaborative plan with processes and goals would be the next logical step. For many libraries, this approach may seem to be overdone or exaggerative, but for those experiencing little or weak collaboration, it may be helpful.

Facilitation may not be a common buzzword and may not often be seen in job descriptions and performance evaluations. To *facilitate* means to make an action easier and provide for smoother paths to completion. Throughout the vignettes in this book, a common thread is how new strategies and ideas can create pathways for library workers to be more efficient and productive. In most cases, a type of barrier was defined and someone has then taken the time to remove or overcome that barrier in some way. Facilitating collaboration involves understanding the culture of the institution or workplace, having a heightened awareness of personnel (which is often associated with workplace information literacy), and using this knowledge to design an intentional plan for collaborating. This is often easier said than done, but it can be good practice to examine how to be a good facilitator in a solution-driven workplace.

Changes that impact the library often have an inordinate effect on collaboration. As seen in the vignette for this chapter, a library was impacted heavily by changes to its hours. The smart solution was to utilize cross-training and analyze processes in order to generate efficiencies and cover the larger workload. While it was fortunate that the library was able to get more staff to cover the new hours, spaces, and services, the analytical approach combined with a good focused exercise ("Shake It Up") made for some good collaborative work in this library.

Full service 24 Hours per Day: Solutions for Effectively Balancing Workloads

JENNIFER HUGHES, Associate University Librarian,
Coastal Carolina University

MICHELLE LEWIS, Manager of Access Services,
Coastal Carolina University

The Kimbel Library of Coastal Carolina University implemented a 24/7 schedule which increased its hours of operation from 92 to 168 per week; an information commons was constructed which increased the library's footprint by 38 percent; and a dual service desk was created to provide both reference and circulation services. To accommodate the growth of hours, space, and services, staffing within the Access Services Department increased from 5 to 19 full-time staff members.

As a result, employees with established work processes and expertise mixed with new employees who lacked departmental knowledge and were unfamiliar with their specific library responsibilities. The existing staff were overworked and territorial of responsibilities, while the new employees were underutilized. In response, supervisors consciously made the decision to implement an uncomfortable "Shake It Up" activity for a full semester. This activity took cross-training to the extreme, and challenged all employees to become immersed in all aspects of the Access Services Department. In addition, the supervisors made a comprehensive list of all departmental activities, and analyzed the optimal time of day for each task to be performed. For example, reconciling the daily finances had been done in the mornings between 8:00 a.m. and 10:00 a.m. by the daytime staff. The staff had to determine if fines had been collected before midnight or afterward for appropriate reconciliation, and they also had to maintain a high level of service for library users preparing for their first class of the day (printing papers, checking out materials, etc.). It made the most sense to move the daily reconciliation of funds to the overnight staff, so they could prepare the deposit just after midnight each day. It also made more sense for shelving and shelf-reading to occur during the overnight hours, when there was less demand for staff to perform circulation transactions at the desk.

Because of the success of the Shake It Up experience, the supervisors proposed a complete organizational overhaul. Instead of having an interlibrary loan (ILL) specialist, circulation specialist, stack maintenance specialist, and so on, every member of the department was given an identical title: Access Services Specialist. Each position description was updated to include an identical set of essential job functions, including providing reference service, processing ILL, performing circulation activities, performing and directing stack maintenance, managing the library facility, handling emergency situations, and supervising student assistants.

The result of a full-service 24/7 library staffed with Access Services Specialists has been phenomenal! The department now has a robust training series to ensure that all employees on each of the three shifts are prepared to provide the highest level of service to library users any time of day, any day of the week. Our library users who need assistance at 3:00 a.m. are able to receive professional support from knowledgeable staff. By devoting a 24-hour team of employees to process ILL requests, our "days to fill" improved from

9.17 to 6.13. The more balanced workloads have had a significant impact on employee morale and the retention of staff. Weekend and overnight employees once felt like they were babysitting the building during their shifts, but now they are fully immersed team members.

In this chapter, collaboration is viewed as an excellent way to overcome library dysfunction. Working together (especially on projects of interest) while balancing workloads and providing adequate time to get work done are all tantamount to good collaborative work. Facilitating diverse teams that have opportunities to bond can also lead to great teamwork. This chapter offers a number of solution-based strategies to help create efficient teams that also embed respectful attitudes towards library workers, and it shows how teams like the one at Coastal Carolina can be put together.

Allow Work on Projects of Interest

Once again, the vignette given here from Coastal Carolina University can be used as a good template for combining staff skills and showing how immersed team members can accomplish a great deal. Although at first, the large increase in hours that the library confronted might not necessarily be considered a "project of interest," the library did a good job of mobilizing the entire library staff for the solution, which heightened their interest level. Exploring what a project of interest may be points to the possibility that individual preferences could possibly work against collaboration.

Some common phrases that echo the notion of allowing workers to work on projects of interest and prosper thereby are "managing to a worker's strengths" and "finding the correct fit." *Fit* is a term that has come under more scrutiny in the current work environment. It has usually been associated more with hiring practices than with finding the right work for current employees, and like many of the other terms we have seen (civility, empathy), it can be used as a type of code word for maintaining the status quo. Meredith Farkas points out that "instead of focusing on hiring people who fit the dominant culture, libraries should explore why others are viewed as bad fits in the first place and how the organization can better appreciate people who don't conform. A critical part of diversity initiatives is inclusion, and organizations will have to look at how welcome and valued everyone is made to feel if they want to improve diversity in the long term."[1] Her post also offers solutions to minimizing bias during hiring.

Interest would appear to be a less loaded word than *fit*. It implies some agency on the part of the worker. Conversely, having a great deal of work to do that does not interest you can obviously impact your job performance in a negative way. To remedy this, are there discussions and initiatives in the library that focus on workers' interests? An easy way to begin these forays would be to get employees talking and sharing. Eamon Tewell advocated for a speed networking event that took place in his library and pointed out that "today's all-staff meeting had a speed networking event where everyone talked with people in different departments to see where our projects intersected. It was fun, and I recommend it for anyone at a large library."[2]

Realistically, there are many daily tasks that do not qualify as projects of interest, yet that should not deter library leaders from soliciting staff suggestions which could lead to work that engages those working in the library.

Provide Adequate Space, Materials, and Time

Inadequate space as a problem in libraries seems to have dissipated to some degree. Although there are certainly libraries that have space issues and see space as a premium, the continued minimization of collection space seems to have affected all libraries positively in some manner. The term *space* may also refer to the design of the workplace environment, which is actually quite a topical issue. One issue currently is the idea of an "open workspace"; that is, instead of private offices, library workers are gathered together, generally in partitioned areas. Like almost any workplace setup, there are plusses and minuses to the open plan. As explored in *The Dysfunctional Library: Challenges and Solutions to Workplace Relationships*, a proportion of 25–35 percent collaborative workspace and 65–75 percent individual workspace, along with some community spaces, is best.[3]

Materials that help make for successful collaboration can vary from library worker to worker. In a general way (depending on how materials are defined), collaboration, or at least the initiation of collaboration, should not take too many materials to occur. Although some consideration must be given to the materials needed for a given project, lack of materials should not necessarily hinder good collaborative endeavors. For example, there are many open-source software options that can facilitate collaboration. Perhaps lack of materials may be a bigger factor when collaborating outside the library, but in many cases this can be met with good teamwork skill sets from librarians and by creative team effort. To summarize, there can be times when a lack of materials can capsize collaborative ventures, but good library leaders and facilitators should be able to overcome these.

Time may be the most important currency in the library workplace, especially in the current environment. In the case of academic libraries, there is a fortunate situation where the year has a cyclical nature and some planning can take place. But each library has its own challenges, and time seems to shrink in much the same way that library budgets do. Time management is obviously an immense topic, so only a brief treatment of the subject is possible here. When considering some of the common narratives about how to optimize time, it can be good practice to find alternative solutions. Referencing the earlier points in this chapter surrounding efficiencies and humane treatment of library workers, topics such as library burnout (Kendrick), vocational awe (Ettarh, discussed in chapter 1), resilience (Tewell), and lifelong learning (Watters) are counter-narratives about power and injustice that can enlighten us. It is up to both library leaders and staffers to take the time to read and educate each other on these different ideas, move away from some commonly held beliefs, and work toward some alternative solutions. As put forth by Veronica Arellano Douglas, "What narratives and ideologies have we bought into our own work in academic libraries? What have we simply accepted as Truth without bothering to question, poke holes in, and dismantle?"[4]

Balance Workloads Equally among Staff

Like many concepts in the workplace, the desired effect can sometimes obscure the difficult work needed to achieve the final goal. In the same way that each library employee could greatly benefit from balancing their own workload as well as balancing their work/home dynamic, it can be a good goal for leaders to try and create balanced workloads among the staff. However, not only is it difficult to come to agreement on what a balanced workload looks like, but it is hard to maintain that workload once it has been achieved. Although a truly consistent balance may not be fully achieved, working to position as many positive aspects in the job as possible in order to compensate for negative ones can be accomplished.

The staff should have a sense that a type of balance and fairness is being attempted. This will encourage staff sustainability, promote high morale, and prevent worker burnout.

Balancing anything takes effort, and in the case where others are involved, it requires a great deal of communicative input from all. This can be especially true for those who have less power and voice in the library. In their blog post "Preparing Early Career Librarians for Leadership and Management: A Feminist Critique," Thomas, Trucks, and Kouns point out that "we need to examine our relationships to and support of oppressive structures not just in the field at large, but within individual libraries. Members of marginalized groups, especially people of color and those who identify as LGBTQIA, experience hidden workloads, microaggressions, early burnout, and lower retention. They have less access to and support for opportunities within their work and leadership roles than their counterparts. The profession can change this by implementing institutional policies for conduct and intervention, prioritizing retention, and incorporating anti-oppression practices into support systems and decision-making."[5] The phrase *hidden workloads* can refer to the work done by many groups who need to go the extra mile to educate others on their situations and serve as representatives on diversity and inclusivity committees. This is another case where considerations that may have gone unnoticed in the past (like vocational awe and power imbalances) need to be thought about when balancing workloads.

The Coastal Carolina vignette once again provides us with ways to increase productivity by leveraging all staff: "By devoting a 24-hour team of employees to process interlibrary loan requests, our days to fill improved from 9.17 to 6.13. The more balanced workloads have had a significant impact on employee morale and retention of staff." Staff sustainability (the retention of good staff) is very often a hallmark of a good library environment that is functioning well, and retaining satisfied staff contributes to high morale and makes staff bonding a rewarding experience.

Conclusion

The Coastal Carolina library vignette gives us an excellent example of how to facilitate collaboration. They met a challenge with a strategy that analyzed the situation, used collaboration and bonding, and then implemented ideas that improved library teamwork. The ability to become efficient was achieved, but not at the cost of alienating library workers or taking anything away from them (in fact, with cross-training they were given more agency). The path this library took could be a good example for all libraries. The additional points made within this chapter such as cross-training, allowing for work on projects of interest, and trying to balance workloads fairly among the staff may provide those who facilitate library collaboration with more robust ideas moving forward.

QUESTIONS FOR REFLECTION

- What type of library projects interest you the most? Have you talked to your library leader about this?
- Do you like the idea of cross-training in your library?
- As a library leader, how do you create an environment in your library that fosters collaboration?
- What types of things can library leaders do to sustain high morale or improve low morale?

NOTES

1. Meredith Farkas, "Is "Fit" a Bad Fit? How Evaluating Job Candidates Can Stifle Diversity," *American Libraries*, https://americanlibrariesmagazine.org/2019/06/03/cultural-fit-bad-fit/.
2. Eamon Tewell, (@EamonTwewll), Twitter, August 14, 2019, 1:31 p.m. https://twitter.com/EamonTewell/status/1161737017140682753.
3. Jo Henry, Joe Eshleman, and Richard Moniz, *The Dysfunctional Library: Challenges and Solutions to Workplace Relationships* (Chicago, IL: ALA, 2018), 129.
4. Veronica Arellano Douglas, "Applying Counter-Narratives to Academic Librarianship," *ACRLog*, 2019, https://acrlog.org/2019/08/22/applying-counter-narratives-to-academic-librarianship/.
5. Camille Thomas, Elia Trucks, and H. B. Kouns, "Preparing Early Career Librarians for Leadership and Management: A Feminist Critique," 2019, *In the Library with the Lead Pipe*, http://www.inthelibrarywiththeleadpipe.org/2019/early-career-leadership-and-management/.

14

Manage Resistance to Change

Resistance to change does not occur exclusively in libraries, of course, but it can be quite pronounced in them. In chapter 10 of *The Dysfunctional Library: Challenges and Solutions to Workplace Relationships*, we suggested that libraries traditionally had a sort of "monopoly" on how information was accessed, but this monopoly was then broken with the rise of the internet. Viewed this way, it is not hard to see why longtime workers at the library would view that time as "the good old days." It has been pointed out, however, that not all aspects of those days were quite as good as some might think. Shirley A. Wiegand and Wayne A. Wiegand point out in *The Desegregation of Public Libraries in the Jim Crow South: Civil Rights and Local Activism* (2018) that "as in other efforts to integrate civic institutions in the 1950s and 1960s, the determination of local activists won the battle against segregation in libraries. In particular, the willingness of young black community members to take part in organized protests and direct actions ensured that local libraries would become genuinely free to all citizens."[1] It is harrowing to think that if everyone in Southern libraries had been resistant to all change, then segregated libraries might still be the norm there.

Of course, not every decision in the library carries as much weight as who has access to the materials. However, as an exercise in exploring resistance to change, it can be illuminating to spend more time with some of the policies and procedures that may be taken for granted within the library. For example, let us examine library fines. Some of the issues surrounding library fines could be ones that were never considered in the past; that is, they present barriers to those who may not be able to afford to pay them. In her TED Talk "A Librarian's Case against Overdue Book Fines," Dawn Wacek sums up how fines present a dilemma for libraries: "On the one hand, we're champions of democracy and we claim that we're there so that every citizen can educate themselves. We're advocates for the power early literacy has to reduce that achievement gap and eliminate the word gap. We tell people, 'We're here to help you.' On the other hand, if you're struggling financially, and you make a mistake, the kind of mistake that anyone in this room could make—your tote bag that belongs to the library sits by your back door for a couple of weeks longer than it should, you lose a CD, you spill your coffee on a book—suddenly, we're not here for you so much anymore, because if that happens, we're going to make you pay for it. And if you can't pay for it, you're out of luck."[2] She goes on to point out how library fines have affected her and how she can afford to pay them while many others cannot. "So is that fair and equitable service if some of us can pay our fines and continue to operate as we always have, and others of us make one mistake and no longer are welcome back? It's simply not."[3] As the divide between rich and poor grows in our society and many of the marginalized are shut out, it would seem as if adding more hurdles to library use such as fines would be something all library workers would want to change. And yet this is not the case, since many libraries continue to fine.

What is interesting about the debate around library fines is that it involves how library staff view and interact with the communities they serve. Libraries are thought of in a positive sense by most people, yet within this good reputation are some barriers than often go unnoticed. For example, library anxiety is a well-documented feeling that inhibits library use. Narrow collections that do not reflect the communities they serve continue to be maintained. As pointed out in chapter 6, the massive imbalance of white library workers has been met with only plodding change. The schism that occurs in libraries around holding on to well-meaning yet often hollow vestiges of the past while trying to change with the times confounds those who wonder if libraries will ever truly mature into what they declare is their commitment to equal access.

Caneda and Green review some of the library literature in their article "Employee Resistance to Change" (2007). They first reference an article by A. Bolognese, who attempts to develop a working definition for the term *resistance*. They then state: "resistance may be defined as a cognitive state, an emotional state, and as a behavior. The cognitive state refers to the negative mindset toward the change. The emotional state addresses the emotional factors, such as frustration and aggression, which are caused by the change. As a behavior, resistance is defined as an action or inaction towards the change. Resistance in any form is intended to protect the employee from the perceived or real effects of change."[4] The idea that resistance can be broken down into a mindset—how one feels and then how one acts—has been applied previously to other dysfunctional attributes such as negative group interactions and poor communication. Many times, the best approach can be to work on the mindset as a start and pay close attention to dispositions (though clear and consistent communication and good listening skills) in order to affect behavior. This tactic can not only be used towards others, but can also be employed when thinking about our own attitudes, feelings, and actions.

In this chapter, understanding the roots and effects of resistance and implementing change will be explored. Then training for new approaches to change mindsets and engage employees in the change process will be discussed. The idea that change occurs constantly will be stressed; because this seems self-evident, we naturally assume that everyone would get accustomed to change and accept it readily. But of course, this is not the case, and it is a bit surprising that those who work in libraries are so reluctant to accept change when libraries have been experiencing change for so long, and it is obvious that these changes will continue to occur in the foreseeable future. Although there are many other fields that have their share of change resisters, it is interesting to consider what it is about librarians that predisposes them to resist change.

Understand Effects and the Roots of Resistance

Instead of using a "head-on" confrontational approach toward those who are resistant to change, it may be a wiser course to attempt to understand why this resistance occurs in the first place. In libraries the common idea is that the resisters are "stuck in the past" and are afraid or even hostile towards ideas that involve constant change. A different approach here would be to listen to those who are reluctant to change. First, however, fully contemplating the word *change* and what it represents may be in order. *Change*, like a great many conceptual words, can have a very expansive meaning. Many articles that address workplace change point out that providing clear information to all affected employees about the type of change that is occurring (or which is about to take place) can help to alleviate a great deal of change resistance.[5]

In examining the root of change resistance, we might ask: what are some of the positives associated with resisting change? One common answer revolves around how many new ideas and changes are proposed. Many library workers can recall a situation where a new procedure, policy, or product is presented as a sort of miraculous answer to a problem, and then this hyped-up vision does not deliver. Obviously, individuals live in a world that competes for attention and the presentation of an idea with minimal fanfare can undermine the attention it gets. So perhaps those who resist change have grown cynical (or in their eyes, wise) about new ideas that are not presented in a balanced way. Additionally, those who feel dubious about change may be outnumbered by a larger group whose members are smitten with each new idea that comes down the pike; in such cases, the former could represent the proverbial "voice of reason." In the study "From Saboteurs to Change Management: Investigating the Correlation between Workplace Behavior and Change Resistance," Young and Dees found that "this study has shown that someone who is resistant to change is not by default a saboteur."[6]

Looking at the library vignette for this chapter, it is easy to pinpoint how thorough and detailed communication, in this case between the library and faculty, can help to minimize change resistance. The roots of resistance in this case stem from a lack of understanding of library policy, and in particular, a lack of appreciation for how weeding can improve a collection, and make more materials attractive for circulation. A final lesson here is how the library learned how to communicate better in the future to affected parties, thereby minimizing the effects of change resistance.

Implementing Change

What qualifies as change in a workplace can be dependent on the ways in which employees react to change. While it may be self-evident that any negative reaction to a change in a library centers on loss of control, there

Managing Change Resistance in a Small Rural Academic Library

REBECCA FREEMAN, Assistant Librarian,
University of South Carolina Lancaster

Change is never an easy thing for an organization or for individuals within that organization. Weeding can be a challenge for any library, especially one in which few changes have been made. I work in a small rural academic library in which few changes had been made to our collection prior to my colleague and myself joining the library. While some weeding had occurred previously, it was done in small steps, and the discarded books were then offered up to faculty and staff to take home.

A couple of years ago, we decided that we needed to go through the collection and pull materials that were damaged and either remove them or repair them. This decision came about because we had noticed that many of our books were damaged, and we wanted to take advantage of the fact that we temporarily had the funds to repair some of these items.

This was a big change from the previous attempts at weeding because (1) we were looking through the whole collection, and (2) we were being required to work with our faculty to determine what materials would stay in the library. We created a set of criteria for what would be pulled from the collection and evaluated. An e-mail was sent to our faculty and staff requesting their feedback on which of these materials should be kept and repaired, and which of them we could safely remove from the collection.

As a result, a situation arose in which we had multiple faculty who stridently wanted to keep every item in the library. Their argument was that we had space on our shelves and libraries should never get rid of anything. Some of the faculty gave us long lists of items that should be repaired instead of removed from the collection. While we were fortunate to have the funds to make some of these repairs, we would not have been able to repair all of the books that had been pulled under the criteria that had been created.

The solution was to work on how we communicated with our faculty and staff. We know that weeding is a challenging topic, so when we spoke with our concerned faculty, we laid out exactly why we were undertaking this task and how we were doing it through the criteria and our Collection Development Policy. In addition, our communication allowed us to demonstrate to the administration that their worries that we would remove items that faculty wanted were unfounded. (Cont.)

The result of this process is that we have been able to successfully carry out two additional weeding events in which we removed materials that were so severely damaged that it was not cost-effective to repair them. Both of these additional events did not meet any resistance from our faculty, and we have been able to show them the importance of cleaning the collection. In addition, it ensured that we have become well-versed in communicating the whys of what we are doing to our administration and faculty.

---

may be a bit more here than meets the eye. For example, there may be an element of fear with regard to change, especially on the part of those who want to "keep the library the same as it always was." Whether consciously or not (and the results are usually the same in either case), there are library employees who want the library to be the same as the one they grew up with. While this nostalgic wistfulness does not appear nefarious at first glance, embedded within it may be other signifiers of how a person is fearful of all change, even when it involves those cherished values that are supported by all libraries. The library worker who harkens back to an earlier, idealized time may be the same one who will not work for inclusion and equality because these ideas are not part of her idealized vision of the library. How does a library leader change this type of attitude?

Catherine B. Soether points out how "a structured process, transparency, and effective communication can assist in making the change easier and the implementation smoother."[7] In her article "Change Management in Libraries: An Essential Competency for Leadership," she concludes that "frank and direct communication may be necessary to bring along employees remaining resistant to the very end. These conversations may be difficult but are essential to the change process and are an essential competency for leadership."[8] Over and over again, in articles, throughout this book, and in our earlier book, good communication triumphs over dysfunction.

Implementing change can require some courageous acts from leaders, especially when a great deal of change is involved. Shifting the discourse from the initial negative reactions to pointing out the positive opportunities can sometimes smooth the path to change. This can be the case with position changes and job responsibilities. Some of the newer library positions such as diversity, equity, and inclusion librarian, student engagement librarian, research engagement and scholarly communication librarian, and digital services librarian show how libraries have grown and tried to provide coverage for new resources and services. Taking a quick look at the different job titles in your library may enable you to quickly assess how much your library resists or accepts change.

Training for New Approaches to Change Mindsets

What is often overlooked, especially by institutions that do not formally assess or periodically review their procedures, is the importance of good training. When dealing with new employees, orientation (or the increasingly popular term *onboarding*) can be extremely important when it comes to supporting new ideas in your library. Conducting an assessment of your library's onboarding practices and the checklists and procedures that new staff are subjected to can be an eye-opening experience. Special attention should be paid to any materials new employees are given which are dated and do not accurately reflect what the library currently wants to achieve. One helpful strategy here would be to inculcate an awareness in new library staff that they can be more actively involved in their own onboarding process in the library. This would be a great way to introduce an idea discussed later in this chapter: getting employees engaged in the change process.

The often-heard lament that librarians are too traditional or are change-resistant may even begin before new library staff are hired. Job descriptions can be the bane of librarians' existence, primarily because these descriptions do not accurately reflect the actual work of the position and fail to present a good picture of librarians' contribution and impact. It would seem at first that job descriptions are the purview of the human resources department, but there is a great deal of variation from library to library in how these descriptions are developed and formulated, and in many cases library employees themselves affect their content.

How could the library train new employees to take new approaches to their positions and think about their job in new ways? One idea would be to try and integrate some of the best ideas that the new librarians are bringing in from previous jobs. Often this occurs organically as the employees settle into their new positions. But once again, bringing this type of idea integration to bear in an intentional way may yield dividends. Steven Bell makes the point that managing issues with change retroactively is not a particularly good tactic. He makes it clear that change is a recurrent phenomenon, and instead of thinking about how to deal with change-resistant library employees, it would be much better to become a "change-ready leader who develops a change-ready culture."[9]

Tyler Walters, the dean of the Virginia Tech Library, has been instrumental in moving his library forward. He says: "We need to be flexible with our expertise and resources and to orient our mindset on the future and where the organization needs to go rather than the current environment. Our goal is to develop the new perspectives and practices that we need to have in place to better serve our community. Setting that tone with employees in the organization is imperative for success."[10] This is how a true leader thinks ahead in order to minimize change resistance. Using communication as a cornerstone, Tyler states: "During the change process, leaders facilitate conversations and help maintain respect and civility within the organization . . . As a leader, it's our job to live in a space that is two to four years away. We help our employees see this world with us and understand their role in the process."[11]

Involving (or not involving) employees in their own changing situations is a good indicator of library functionality. Library workers who have change sprung on them or who feel left out of the process are surely in a dysfunctional situation, one marked by a power imbalance, insecure leadership, the makings of a coming crisis, or various other problems. The proverbial tip of the dysfunctional iceberg can be seen when library employees have no awareness or agency when it comes to changes in the library.

Engage Employees in the Change Process

As mentioned previously, involving employees in the changes that impact them is of the utmost importance. In tandem with poor communication, a feeling of "being left out" can really damage an employee's morale. Low morale in libraries has been examined in great detail by Kaetrena Davis Kendrick. In her article "The Low Morale Experience of Academic Librarians: A Phenomenological Study,"[12] she presents the situations of many library workers who suffer from numerous indignities and often find themselves working in a library without purpose.

While it makes perfect sense to see a connection between dysfunction and low morale, each of these problems does have some distinctive elements of its own. Dysfunction primarily involves how the library performs (although how the employees interact with each other certainly contributes to a library's functionality), while employee morale can be gauged a bit more easily. Library employees who are frustrated and anxious and who feel they are not accomplishing anything may be easy to spot, but quite difficult to help. Certainly, many employees can point to some aspect of their jobs that seems quite fruitless and doesn't appear to have any purpose. But imagining that your entire job felt this way should give you some insight into an employee with low morale feels.

Some examples of ways to engage employees in the change process, with particular attention to library work, involve exercises such as brainstorming sessions and team-bonding exercises. Leaders can hold meetings, events, and group gatherings and embed the idea of change within these opportunities. Taking (and implementing) suggestions is a good way to involve employees. Another effective approach is to point out any changes that have been made in response to past surveys which asked library workers for feedback or advice, show how these earlier ideas from staff were implemented, and how this feedback helped the library.

Conclusion

The one constant is change, and though this truism does little for those who are resistant to change, it does offer the idea that each of us accepts change to some degree. While every experienced librarian has gone through change and has mainly moved on in some way with it, this lesson of adaptability often gets lost when the next change rolls around. Still, those resistant to change most likely evolve to the point in their careers where they accept some change, because as noted above, change is occurring almost all of the time. Whether it is new personnel, new policies, new patrons, or new products, each librarian experiences some type of change at some point during the year. While it is overstating it to say that resistance to change is everywhere, it may be accurate to say that those who embrace positive change are actively battling dysfunction.

QUESTIONS FOR REFLECTION

- Are librarians really resistant to change, or is that an unproven stereotype or myth?
- Are there times in your library when those who resisted a change were proven correct, and in hindsight, they should have been listened to more closely?
- When discussing changing something in your library, such as eliminating fines, do most of the decisions revolve around how the change impacts your community or how it affects staff? Or does it concern something else, such as policy or the power structures within the library?

NOTES

1. Wayne A. Wiegand and Shirley A. Wiegand, *The Desegregation of Public Libraries in the Jim Crow South: Civil Rights and Local Activism* (Baton Rouge, LA: LSU Press, 2018).
2. Dawn Wacek, "A Librarian's Case against Overdue Book Fines," TED Ideas Worth Spreading, 2018, https://www.ted.com/talks/dawn_wacek_a_librarian_s_case _against_overdue_book_fines?language=en.
3. Wacek, "A Librarian's Case against Overdue Book Fines."
4. Suzanne Caneda and Ravonne Green, "Employee Resistance to Change," *Library Worklife: HR E-News for Today's Leaders*, 2007, http://ala-apa.org/newsletter/2007/ 11/16/employee-resistance-to-change/.
5. Joyce E.A. Russell, "How to Create Change in the Workplace," *Washington Post,* WP Company, Dec. 1, 2013, www.washingtonpost.com/business/capitalbusiness/ how-to-create-change-in-the-workplace/2013/11/27/9d62f8de-5548-11e3 -835de7173847c7cc_story.html; Glenn Llopis, "Change Management Requires Leadership Clarity and Alignment," *Forbes,* June 30, 2014, www.forbes.com/sites/ glennllopis/2014/06/30/change-management-requires-leadership-clarity -and-alignment/#5502b3ee3e3c; Tim Creasey, "The Correlation Between Change Management and Project Success," *Prosci* (blog), https://blog.prosci.com/the-correla tion-between-change-management-and-project-success.
6. Brian Young and Ashley Dees, "From Saboteurs to Change Management: Investigating the Correlation between Workplace Behavior and Change Resistance," 2007, Association of College & Research Libraries, http://www.ala.org/acrl/sites/ ala.org.acrl/files/content/conferences/confsandpreconfs/2017/FromSaboteurs toChangeManagement.pdf.
7. Catherine B. Soehner, "Change Management in Libraries: An Essential Competency for Leadership," Proceedings of the IATUL Conferences, 2014, https://docs.lib .purdue.edu/cgi/viewcontent.cgi?article=2059&context=iatul.
8. Soehner, "Change Management in Libraries."
9. Steven Bell, "From Change Management to Change-Ready Leadership | Leading from the Library," *Library Journal*, March 1, 2018, https://www.libraryjournal .com/?detailStory=change-management-change-ready-leadership-leading-library.
10. "University Libraries Dean Tyler Walters Discusses Leadership and Change Management," Virginia Tech Daily, 2018, https://vtnews.vt.edu/articles/2018/11/ univlib-walters-charlestonconference.html.
11. "University Libraries Dean Tyler Walters Discusses Leadership and Change Management."
12. Kaetrena Davis Kendrick and Ione T. Damasco, "The Low-Morale Experience of Minority Academic Librarians: A Review," Prezi, 2019, https://prezi.com/ pqawnmki_foy/the-low-morale-experience-of-minority-academic-librarians-a-review/.

PART IV

The Functional Organization

15

Assemble and Hire the Right Library Staff

Perhaps nothing is more important for a library manager or leader than hiring the right people. In addition to the potential loss in productivity, a bad hire can be corrosive in any library. Thus, the emphasis in this chapter will be on the critical importance of soft skills, fit, and encouraging diversity.

According to Anne Barnhart et al., "Most librarian job searches do not measure the 'soft skills' that have become a vital aspect of almost every working environment, not just the library."[1] This needs to change. The modern library requires its staffers to have excellent interpersonal skills. It is the rare position that does not, for example, interact with patrons on some level. Even individuals working behind the scenes will do so on occasion and must also interact with other staff as well. Collaboration, both within and outside the library, is essential. Libraries can no longer be separate, stand-alone entities. They need to be integrated into their schools, institutions, and communities in ways that were not as imperative in the past. In one study that considered the ideal attributes of academic library directors, Gary Fitsimmons states: "Academic administrators felt more strongly about the personal attributes category than the others, especially integrity and the ability to work collaboratively with other campus colleagues."[2] This could readily be applied to positions beyond just that of a director or senior library administrator. In fact, in most library jobs, it is not sufficient to have the ability to work with others; you must *thrive* on it.

Another important trait in hiring is drive. We need to seek out individuals who want to earn the respect of their colleagues through effort and hard work. In referring to the U.S. Marine Corps, David Snyder says: "It seems that what the Marines are looking for is what everyone is looking for: a group of people who have an innate desire to prove themselves— people who do not feel that they deserve this and that, but people who would like to have the opportunity to demonstrate their worth. Such candidates, as any employer will tell you, are increasingly in the minority."[3] One suspects that Snyder's negative references here reflect the commonly held belief (or prejudice?) that younger generations seem less inclined to start somewhere and then work their way up. Fitsimmons's study isolated some key attributes sought in academic library directors. These may be applied to other positions as well, such as "being learning/student centered, having a strong work ethic, the ability to work effectively with all campus constituent groups [or all members of a community or school], a positive personality, and compatibility with the institutional mission."[4] This highlights the importance of collaboration, but it also relates to the fundamental mission of libraries, to educate and inform. It additionally speaks to the kind of positive, "can do" spirit that is needed to work in an environment undergoing rapid change and transformation. According to Bruce Massis, "It is imperative not only that employees learn to adapt to each other, but also that they enter the workplace each day with a positive attitude that can be adopted throughout the entire workplace environment."[5] Anne Barnhart et al. phrase this as being "focused on finding new colleagues who could navigate uncertainty while being flexible and good-natured."[6] These authors are not saying that employees should see everything with rose-colored glasses, but that they should be equipped to handle difficulties and setbacks. This kind of attitude can be ascertained, at least to some degree, in the hiring process.

SOME QUALITIES TO LOOK FOR WHEN HIRING

- Integrity
- Responsibility
- Compassion
- Ability to forgive
- Empathy
- Drive
- Adaptability

Even before a hiring need arises, library leaders should be making connections and scouting for talent. Gauri Sharma aptly advises: "Network, even when you do not have an open position."[7] LIS instructors, library professionals, and library administrators enjoy interacting with new librarians and enjoy meeting veteran library staffers. This is helpful when one needs to fill a position. Many libraries take on LIS interns. In addition to the internship itself, which benefits both students and the library, these individuals often become candidates for open positions. When considering the potential vagaries of the hiring process, it is good to get some applicants who have already proven themselves in the setting in which they are being hired.

The hiring process often begins with an internal procedure that seeks administrative approval to fill an open position. The hiring itself then begins with the posted job description. According to Fitsimmons, "The vacancy announcement is your first contact with each candidate, and as such should be designed to make a great (but honest) first impression."[8] Job descriptions should provide some detail about the type of work required in the position, the necessary and preferred qualifications of the applicant, and the type of environment existent at the library doing the hiring. The description should also contain a salary range. There is nothing more frustrating than wasting everyone's time when an applicant has no way of telling if there is a significant mismatch in this regard. It seems self-evident, but many job descriptions are sorely lacking on one or more of these points. An ideal organization allows hiring managers to proactively write job descriptions that meet all these requirements, provide applicants with a great first impression of the library, and describe in detail the work the position entails. Unfortunately, other, less savvy organizations simply post to lowest common denominators such as "Proficiency in Microsoft Office Word."

In pursuing talent, you should be prepared to move quickly to get the best candidates. According to Emily Weak, "Some organizations take months to hire, some take weeks."[9] Unfortunately, in academia, most organizations take the former as opposed to the latter. It is not unheard of for a hiring process to take a full year. Surely, many excellent applicants have moved on to other things by then.

When sorting candidates, an important consideration is negotiable factors. For example, the library has an opening for an entry-level librarian position that requires an MLIS. The automated system itself may be set to screen out anyone who does not meet this qualification. What if, in screening applicants this way, someone who is just a month or two away from finishing their MLIS and would be an ideal candidate, is missed? This may be an extreme example, but it is important to think about what is wanted. This could work the other way as well. For example, a part-time position is posted that requires the successful candidate to be flexible on which evenings they can work, but this requirement is not included in the posting or in early conversations with applicants. Unfortunately, this could waste everyone's time by bringing in unsuitable candidates.

After promising applicants are identified, the next step is usually a preliminary interview by phone or by synchronous teleconferencing technology. This can entail a committee or could be done by a single individual. At this stage, most administrators prefer the latter, usually taking up the task themselves or selectively allowing other staff to lead the way. There are advantages to using teleconferencing applications, but a phone conversation can also be very rich as well. According to Fitsimmons, a phone call has many advantages over e-mail communication and can provide a better understanding of an individual because it requires spontaneity and instant back-and-forth communication.[10] It is not recommended to surprise someone with a phone call, but once it is set up, some basic questions should be ready. This is a good opportunity to describe any aspects of the position that were not elaborated in the posting. It is also a good opportunity to see what the candidate is looking for. The candidate's tone can show enthusiasm, while hesitation can imply diffidence. For example, when asked if she can work certain shifts or take on certain tasks, the applicant's response time and tone of voice will often hint at how sure she is in her response.

Despite their usefulness, phone conversations and Skype interviews obviously have serious limitations and should only be used in the screening process and preliminary interviews. Different institutions apply different rules as to how many candidates to bring in to the library for interviews. Generally speaking, public libraries tend to be stricter in this regard. While some libraries may bring in 4 or 5 candidates, the norm tends to be 3. This gives the search committee some choices and points of comparison and yet does not overburden the staff's time. In some institutions, the interview process can last a long time, even as long as several days.

How should in-person interviews be conducted so that the library can end up selecting the best person for the job? According to Richaurd Camp, "The most effective strategies include developing and using an interviewer guide, previewing the interview process for the candidate, probing to gather more complete behavioral data, reinforcing the impression you want to create, managing the interviewing environment, and streamlining the interview process with team interviews."[11] A list of primary questions that will be asked should first be in place. Camp warns about using different questions for applicants: "Interviewers who have not structured their process are also likely to ask different questions of different candidates. As a result, the interviewers will not necessarily use the same standards to assess all applicants for the same position."[12] This is an important consideration in order to have a fair process. While the chair of the search committee should lead the way, other committee members should be included in the process of determining the most useful questions to ask. Rick Jetter, along with others, encourages the use of rubrics, in addition to narratives or storytelling, in order to obtain the most useful information about the applicant.[13] According to Brannon and Leuzinger, "Because one is trying to express qualitative information in essentially a quantitative manner, creating the descriptors that indicate each level of performance distinctly may take time . . . At the very least, everyone on an interview team should be knowledgeable on how each criteria is defined, and how to glean information from the candidate."[14]

An interview should always begin by providing introductions and setting the candidate at ease. It is never easy to be interviewed, and the goal is to make the person feel comfortable about revealing who they are. Only then can both sides determine if there is a good fit. Additionally, it is important not to sugarcoat any challenges in the job or the workplace. If the library has faced budget cuts or is experiencing difficulties, these should be tactfully conveyed. Lastly, it is worth sharing a point made by John C. Daresh: "All must understand that they, by law, may not question candidates about the following:

- Marital status
- Family issues (for example, if they have children)
- Sexual orientation
- Religion
- Physical condition
- Any other background information concerning matters totally unrelated to an applicant's ability to perform any or all duties related to the job"[15]

Storytelling should be a required element in the interview process. Why? According to Barnhart et al., "Storytelling reveals more about the perspective, worldview, and emotional intelligence of the candidate than do closed questions . . . Framing a response within a story reveals much more about the narratives one might choose to retain and the attitude one had about the experience."[16] Asking someone to elaborate on their qualities or simply regurgitate their experience point by point may not provide much insight into their thinking or problem-solving skills, but asking them to elaborate on a project they worked on can be surprisingly informative. What was the most successful project they worked on? Did they share credit for the project? Did they overcome obstacles? What projects were they involved in that failed or were less than successful? Did they push blame onto others or circumstances entirely, or do they take ownership of their mistakes?

Other questions can provide useful information, not just for the interview, but also for the ongoing management of this potential staff member. Barnhart suggests "Asking interviewees to describe the best and worst bosses they ever had to reveal important attitudes about managers and management."[17] In other cases they were "asked to describe the supportive and non-supportive work environments they had experienced. They were also asked what could have made the non-supportive environment better and how they saw themselves contributing to a supportive environment."[18] Probing for the candidate's areas of internal motivation may also bring insight. Finally, Gauri Sharma suggests "simulat[ing] a day-to-day task . . . to gauge [the candidate's] strengths in action."[19]

Some final process suggestions include not scheduling candidate interviews back to back. Aside from the potentially awkward nature of doing this, committee members can easily start mixing up their impressions of candidates. A best practice is to have at least some debriefing with the committee after each candidate has left the library. Once a final decision is made, have the professionalism to contact each of the applicants who has applied and thank them for their interest. An e-mail is sufficient, but a phone call is more appropriate for those who came in to interview.

Diversity

Diversity deserves special treatment here. Sarah Larsen says: "According to the most recent data published by the American Library Association (ALA), 87.1 percent of librarians identify as white and 81.0 percent identify as female. The populations being served by public libraries are steadily becoming more and more diverse, but the library workforce remains predominantly white and female and bears little relationship to the populations served. According to the ALA, a mere 4.3 percent of librarians are black, 3.5 percent are Asian, and 3.7 percent identify as 'other.'"[20] Clearly, our profession does not yet mirror those we serve. Larsen further notes: "It also means understanding that recruitment of a talented and diverse workforce is difficult due to low salaries in the field compared to other industries, which are rooted in the historical undervaluing of women's work."[21] Furthermore, according to Angela Galvan, "librarianship is paralyzed by whiteness. This will continue unabated without interrogating structures that benefit white librarians, including the performative nature of recruitment and hiring."[22] Sensoy and DiAngelo's article entitled "'We Are All for Diversity, but . . .': How Faculty Hiring Committees Reproduce Whiteness, and Practical Suggestions for How They Can Change" is an excellent deep dive into the topic, especially for anyone hiring in academic libraries. They poignantly state: "Rather than exempt ourselves from the lack of change, we must consider the inevitability of our complicity. Our task, then, is to identify how our complicity is manifesting, rather than to establish our so-called openness or neutrality."[23] These deep-rooted problems have not been easy to solve despite efforts on the part of the American Library Association and other organizations. There is much evidence to suggest that diverse organizations are more successful.[24] So how do library organizations get there?

One of the easiest things to do from the outset is to diversify the search committees when interviewing and hiring. Sarah Larsen notes, "To combat this bias, an easy strategy is to ensure hiring decisions are made by more than one person, and preferably a diverse group of people."[25] Galvan provides some additional suggestions, such as:

- Offer flexible times for internships. Requiring specific availability is the prerogative of the library, but understand that this limits the diversity of your applicant pool. Partial or fully virtual internships offer tremendous opportunities for the library to expand as a truly 24-hour entity.
- Screen interview notes for biased language.
- Noting that the applicant "doesn't seem professional" without articulating why is a problem.
- When someone says "I just like them better," find out why.
- When seeking marginalized employees to serve on diversity, hiring, or outreach committees, consider if this is the only kind of service work they are asked to do. Consistently asking the same people to perform emotional labor causes burnout and suggests the organization is not listening to marginalized staff.

Diversity Efforts at the Atkins Library, UNC Charlotte

DENELLE EADS, Associate Professor,
Atkins Library, University of North Carolina Charlotte

The Atkins Library at the University of North Carolina Charlotte has tried to address diversity and inclusion as we move forward in growing and diversifying our library staff. We recognize that any type of change in an organization takes time, as well as a supportive staff that is willing to accept change. Getting buy-in and obtaining the trust and confidence of our staff depend heavily on how diversity initiatives are integrated into our organization. Since diversity is a delicate issue, I believe that constructing a well-thought-out plan for diversity efforts is essential to successful implementation. This is why the Atkins Library chose to ease into the idea of diversifying our staff by taking gradual steps that would lead to our overall goal of a diverse workplace. This translates into ensuring that diversity, equity, and inclusion are reflected in our mission, practices, and strategic planning, as well as our hiring and retention initiatives. These steps include educating our current staff and heightening their awareness of what embracing diversity actually means. As I mentioned, diversity is a delicate subject that elicits all sorts of reactions from all types of people. In the workplace, diversity requires a level of unified understanding among staff, especially when many staff view the subject through different lenses. We all have personal experiences that affect how we feel about diversity, and this fact should be recognized in the workplace. Just as the word *diversity* means different things to different people, defining what diversity is in the workplace should be viewed the same way. When staff are on the same page about how the organization defines diversity and they understand what diversity means collectively for the entire organization, progress, acceptance, and buy-in for diversity initiatives will occur.

In the Atkins Library, we strove for a unified level of understanding by initiating conversations and offering workshops, programs, and events that focus on the topics of diversity, inclusion, and equity and their importance in the workplace. I believe that learning from others and educating others is key in helping to create a healthy and welcoming work environment that supports and embraces workplace diversity. When staff are exposed to or informed about how people have differences that require acknowledgment, the various kinds of communication, dialogue, and engagement that ensue heighten the awareness of the members of our organization, and they are more ready to embrace our diversity and inclusion initiatives. Communicating and talking about delicate and sensitive issues opens minds, which in turn helps people to accept change in an organization. In our case, discussing diversity issues allowed members of our organization to gain awareness about the importance of the inclusion of all people. Educating a staff, in my opinion, is a crucial aspect in promoting diversity, equity, and inclusion in an organization. For me, diversifying a workplace is like building a house. One needs to build a foundation first before anything can be set in place. A carpenter cannot expect to build the roof of a house until there is a foundation of floors, walls, and ceilings. The Atkins Library began building a foundation of diversity efforts by setting up a few building blocks.

Forming a Diversity & Inclusion Committee in our library was our first step. This committee, comprised of both faculty and staff members, met to discuss the only item on the agenda, "diversity." With no specific guidelines or direction, members began sharing stories with each other and reflecting on personal experiences that resonated with them, which encompassed the broad scope of what diversity involves: race, religion, gender, disability, and so on. Our first committee meeting was a powerful vehicle. It was eye-opening to hear others share various perspectives on diversity. Out of the success of this meeting grew the first diversity activity for our library, a forum called "Conversations That Matter" that allowed Atkins Library employees to participate in discussions about diversity, inclusion, and equity.

After our first "Conversations That Matter," our staff got on board and began participating in other diversity activities sponsored by our Diversity & Inclusion Committee. These activities included a Micro and Macro Aggression workshop, Webinars on Unbiased Consciousness, Racial and Equity forums, and a Diversity Day program, which helped to further educate our organization on what embracing diversity is all about.

Having a diverse workforce is something that will not happen overnight—it takes time and tools to build a strong foundation to achieve such an organizational change. After several years of building our foundation, the Atkins Library is proud to have a subcommittee, formed from the Diversity & Inclusion Committee, which focuses specifically on assessing our practices of recruitment, hiring, and retention of candidates from underrepresented groups. In addition, the library recently received funding to hire a Diversity Resident Librarian, which takes us one step closer to our goal, having a diverse workforce.

Nepotism and Cronyism

One big challenge to diversity can be the issues of nepotism and cronyism, although these problems are not quite as clear-cut as one would think. Nepotism raises many issues, including a potential lack of diversity as well as negative perceptions, even when highly qualified candidates are chosen. One study indicates that "people have negative attitudes toward nepotism and they stigmatize those who benefit from a family connection in the hiring process by perceiving them less favorably. We found that compared to merit-based hires, nepotism hires had less competence attributed to them, and their successful performance was seen as being less due to ability and effort than was the case for merit hires."[26] In cases where a nepotistic hire is made, it is recommended that all team members be made aware of the bona fide credentials and experience of the person hired.

Cronyism is a variation of nepotism. It refers to hiring individuals based on some prior relationship with a member or members of the search committee, not one that is familial. If staff are networking on a regular basis, they may very well identify talent outside the organization that would be beneficial to bring in. It would be foolish to deny the knowledge of committee members in this respect. But like nepotism, an individual hired because of their connections might have to deal with resentment from other staffers. Again, it is important that if such a hire is made, team members should be made to understand the qualifications of that person's job-related skills and experience. According to Shaheen, Bashir, and Khan, "The practice of cronyism poses great challenges for those employees who are committed to their organization and have put in a lot of energy to carry out organizational tasks, yet they are denied of promotions, respectful treatment, and advancement opportunities due to organizational cronyism."[27] Leadership needs to make sure that cronyism is carefully and transparently considered within the hiring process and beyond. According to Shaheen, Bashir, and Abdul Khan, one "way to reduce organizational cronyism is support from top management for merit-based practices."[28]

Conclusion

Hiring is one of the most important things that libraries do. It is important that the process is deliberate. Specific types of interviews can lead to obtaining better information about candidates. Furthermore, it is important to involve a wide variety of staff and perspectives in order to recruit a more diverse, inclusive, and successful library team.

QUESTIONS FOR DISCUSSION

- What does the hiring process at your library look like?
- How would you improve the hiring process at your library?
- What would an ideal hiring process in your library look like?
- How does your library seek to remove bias in the selection process?
- How can you recruit a more diverse team?

NOTES

1. Anne C. Barnhart et al., "The Fit Test: Interview Techniques to Build a Strong Team," in *Advances in Librarianship* (Bingley, UK: Emerald Group, 2014), 156.
2. Gary Neil Fitsimmons, "Academic Library Directors in the Eyes of Hiring Administrators: A Comparison of the Attributes, Qualifications, and Competencies Desired by Chief Academic Officers with Those Recommended by Academic Library Directors," in *Advances in Library Administration and Organization* (Bingley, UK: Emerald Group, 2008), 306.
3. David Snyder, *How to Hire a Champion: Insider Secrets to Find, Select, and Keep Great Employees* (Newburyport, MA: Career, 2008), 54.
4. Fitsimmons, "Academic Library Directors in the Eyes of Hiring Administrators," 306.
5. Bruce Massis, "Hiring for Attitude and Training for Skill in the Library," *New Library World* 116, no. 7/8 (2015): 468.
6. Barnhart et al., "The Fit Test," 160.
7. Gauri Sharma, "How to Grow a Small Team: Nine Hiring Best Practices," *Forbes*, May 21, 2013, https://www.forbes.com/sites/gaurisharma/2013/05/21/how-to-grow-a-small-team-nine-hiring-best-practices/#6cd6a3194aca.
8. Gary Fitsimmons, "Directing the Personnel Search Part I: The Position Announcement," *The Bottom Line* 23, no. 4 (2010): 205–7.
9. Emily Weak, "What Candidates Want: How to Practice Compassionate Hiring," *Library Leadership & Management* 28, no. 4 (2014): 2.
10. Gary Fitsimmons, "Directing the Personnel Search Part II: Notes on Contacting Applicants," *The Bottom Line* 24, no. 1 (2011): 38–40.
11. Richaurd Camp et al., *Strategic Interviewing: How to Hire Good People* (Somerset, NJ: John Wiley & Sons, 2001), 119.
12. Camp et al., *Strategic Interviewing,* 190.

13. Rick Jetter, *Hiring the Best Staff for Your School: How to Use Narrative to Improve Your Recruiting Process* (Indianapolis, IN: Routledge, 2016), 50.

14. Sian Brannon and Julie Leuzinger, "Keeping Human Resources Happy: Improving Hiring Processes through the Use of Rubrics," *Library Leadership & Management* 29, no. 1 (December 2014): 3, 5, http://search.ebscohost.com/login.aspx?direct=true&db=lii&AN=99529325&site=ehost-live&scope=site.

15. John C. Daresh and Bridget Daresh, *How to Interview, Hire, and Retain High-Quality New Teachers* (Bloomington, IN: Solution Tree, 2012), 28.

16. Barnhart et al., "The Fit Test," 161.

17. Barnhart et al., "The Fit Test," 160.

18. Barnhart et al., "The Fit Test," 161.

19. Sharma, "How to Grow a Small Team."

20. Sarah Larsen, "Diversity in Public Libraries: Strategies for Achieving a More Representative Workforce," *Public Libraries* 56, no. 3 (May 2017): 32.

21. Larsen, "Diversity in Public Libraries," 34.

22. Angela Galvan, "Soliciting Performance, Hiding Bias: Whiteness and Librarianship," *In the Library with the Lead Pipe*, June 3, 2015, http://www.inthelibrarywiththeleadpipe.org/2015/soliciting-performance-hiding-bias-whiteness-and-librarianship/.

23. Özlem Sensoy and Robin DiAngelo, "'We Are All for Diversity, but . . .': How Faculty Hiring Committees Reproduce Whiteness, and Practical Suggestions for How They Can Change," *Harvard Educational Review* 87, no. 4 (2017): 577.

24. Larsen, "Diversity in Public Libraries," 34.

25. Larsen, "Diversity in Public Libraries," 34.

26. Margaret Padgett, Robert Padgett, and Kathryn Morris, "Perceptions of Nepotism Beneficiaries: The Hidden Price of Using a Family Connection to Obtain a Job," *Journal of Business Psychology* 30 (2015): 294.

27. Sadia Shaheen, Sajid Bashir, and Abdul Karim Khan, "Examining Organizational Cronyism as an Antecedent of Workplace Deviance in Public Sector Organizations," *Public Personnel Management* 46, no. 3 (September 2017): 317.

28. Shaheen, Bashir, and Khan, "Examining Organizational Cronyism," 318.

16

Provide Organizational Structure

ibraries are in a state of rapid change. This presents us with an array of both opportunities and challenges. According to Reggie Raju et al., "At no time in the history of academic librarianship have libraries been so vulnerable with regard to becoming redundant. Paradoxically, there is so much potential to become noteworthy partners or collaborators in the evolving teaching and learning and research processes of the sector."[1] Raju et al. go on to state: "In this changing paradigm, librarians are harnessing their learning and knowledge to loosen their attachment to buildings and collections and are developing themselves as collaborators in ways external to the physical space."[2]

As libraries look to add new services and explore new solutions, library leaders need to keep in mind that simply adding new technology and services is not enough. According to Nazarzadeh Zare, "Nowadays, successful organizations in the world are the ones which allow change and transformation within their institutional framework."[3] Furthermore, Ronald C. Jantz asserts that "the structure of the organization should change to adapt to and align with various factors in the external environment."[4] In many ways, it is the external environment and the changes it has brought about which have provided libraries with the greatest challenges. Jantz duly notes that "the ambidextrous orientation of the organization is characterized by the ability to simultaneously conduct exploratory activities while also supporting and enhancing current services."[5] This is a key point, since library organizations must find a balance between the needs of their patrons both today and tomorrow. As stated by school library media specialist Lisa Moniz, "We must prepare our patrons to adapt to a future that we cannot predict."[6]

As changes are considered in services and structures, libraries must not forget their most important asset, the staff. In reporting on a recent public library-related study, Diane Velasquez notes that "everyone interviewed had stories about resistance to change. Many of them talked about people who retired rather than deal with automation when catalogs were initially computerized."[7] She goes on to state that "technology was accompanied by staff turnover. Some of the staff left because they chose not to adapt to the new technology. For others, it was just time to move on to new things." Likewise, J. Stephen Town notes: "The literature suggests that high levels of emotion in the workplace are likely at times of disruptive change, and especially when there is a sense that some staff groups are worse off than others, and consequently perceive injustice in their treatment."[8] This can be a considerable problem when a library is shifting its structures and workflows and redefining its services. In considering staff, one element of primary importance is to remember that changes to technology, services, and organization "require new services and skills."[9]

Libraries have a history of evolving. According to Town, "Libraries have a strong track record of measuring performance and using data and evidence to improve their services."[10] In academic libraries especially, there has been an ever-increasing need to provide data in order to encourage, support, and evaluate change. This data, in turn, has informed new and improved planning processes. For example, Camille Andrews et al. note: "Increasingly, planning and outreach strategies are focused on changing from preprogrammed areas and services designed to serve librarian-defined needs to an open and flexible architecture that better incorporates and facilitates the projects, ideas, and interest-driven learning initiated by users."[11]

Library organizations also need to be deliberate. Invoking the work of Peter Drucker, Jantz notes that innovation should become systemically embedded into the way staff get things done, not just a one-off innovation here and there.[12] While this indicates a potentially positive change in focus, it does not immediately offer specific solutions.

Workload Issues and Budget Cuts

When exploring organizational restructuring and new solutions, two important considerations need to be addressed. These are critical from a staff perspective. Many libraries struggle with balancing the workload of staff, and it is the rare library which has not suffered from budget cuts. According to Anne Ford, "A $16 million budget shortfall led the University of Southern Maine to lay off 50 faculty and 100 staff members and eliminate several departments a few years ago. As for the library, it was told to slice 10% of its budget— about $380,000."[13] Unfortunately, the University of Southern Maine seems to be the rule rather than the exception. In fact, even Ivy League institutions have found themselves unable to sustain some services. Beverly Goldberg reports that even at the Harvard University Libraries, budget cuts led to the "mandated realignment of 73 libraries into streamlined reporting structures and shared services."[14] Likewise, she notes the situation at UC Berkeley: "With the loss of public funding at Berkeley over the past four years, the Library has lost over 70 budgeted staff, equivalent to more than 20% of our budgeted positions."[15] Reporting on cuts at the UCT Libraries (in Cape Town, South Africa), Raju notes, "This expectation meant that hard choices had to be made between maintaining traditional services and adopting new ones."[16]

So while it is an exciting time to be working in libraries, it can be difficult as well. Some libraries have been frustrated by the dual need to cut budgets and add hours and services.[17] This requires difficult choices. Ford reports an instance, for example, where a library administrator "cut back on services rather than spread herself and her staff even thinner."[18] Pixey Mosley warns of the danger of creeping responsibilities as one rises through the library ranks. According to her, "Most formal position descriptions have somewhere between 2% and 10% assigned to a category generally defined as 'Other Duties as Assigned' or a similar broadly written phrase . . . As one takes on titled leadership roles, one will see a significant increase in how much time is spent on activities that fall into the 'Other Duties as Assigned.'"[19] It is worth noting one solution that is available to leaders, according to Mosley: "A leader who is comfortable dealing with the messy situations passed up to them will make staff members feel supported and confident in their own abilities, and the staff will know there are options available for the overwhelming situations. Similarly, actively pitching in during a crisis, rather than directing from behind a desk, sends a clear message of teamwork, investment, and valuing contributions."[20] Leaders need to be seen as leading by example.

Restructuring in Library Organizations

When one refers to libraries and change, thoughts about reorganizing and restructuring are commonplace. These terms refer to the way in which a library's hierarchy or organizational chart is set up to accomplish stated goals. It is important to review and develop a library's structures over time.

Exploring the structure of library services begins with patrons. This is one reason why ethnography has recently been more widely employed in libraries.[21] Studying the behavior of patrons as they interact with library services, resources, and facilities provides rich data as the basis for implementing change. Another less radical approach that has seen widespread implementation in larger libraries is the creation of a position or department that is focused on user experiences. For example, at the Albert R. Mann Library at Cornell University, considering the user perspective "led to the creation of the User Engagement Librarian position that is responsible for space, service, and technology assessment and outreach to users."[22] Likewise, according to Bruce L. Keisling, "Engaging users and understanding their needs and preferences in Ekstrom and the University Libraries took on a new life early in 2013 with the recruitment of a dedicated assessment/user experience librarian."[23] Mark E. de Jong paints an even more urgent picture: "Quite simply, libraries that do not investigate SD [service design] methods and implement community-specific design strategies may begin to suffer patron dissatisfaction and even lose patronage."[24]

Using Data at UNCC to Make Decisions

BECKY CROXTON, Head of Assessment,
J. Murrey Atkins Library, University of North Carolina Charlotte

The J. Murrey Atkins Library at the University of North Carolina Charlotte has an assessment team comprised of the head of assessment, the user experience librarian, and an assessment analyst. Too often, library decision-making is based on emotion and hunches. The Atkins Library assessment team works to minimize this by prioritizing the patron experience above all else. We do this through thoughtful and purposeful data-gathering and analyses, including talking to patrons about their needs and preferences, observing their behavior, conducting surveys, and compiling usage statistics related to our collections, services, and spaces. Together, these approaches allow us to create a robust set of data that the library uses to make informed decisions. In fact, our assessment team is currently helping to drive a complete redesign of our library website that focuses upon the user experience. We have gathered and analyzed an enormous set of qualitative and quantitative data relating to our website, including interviews with students and faculty about their information needs and preferences, survey data about how students use the library site, Google Analytics data to inform us about the most frequent uses of our site, card-sorting and tree-testing data related to site navigation and information architecture, and usability testing data about how patrons perform tasks on our site. Together, this triangulated data set is enabling the library's website redesign team to create prototypes to share with our patrons for continued testing and refinement. While we recognize that our website will "never be done," we are confident that what we develop will be useful and usable, and user-centered.

Once the library services being provided are better understood, the next step is to consider what goes on behind the scenes to provide those services. According to Arja Juntunen, "In developing a service organization, it is important to understand the significance of the internal processes which produce services."[25] Likewise, as stated by Camille Andrews, "Apart from user satisfaction and logistically making the experience of the library as seamless as possible, how could spaces impact student learning, staff productivity, and faculty research, and how can that be assessed?"[26] While focused on academic libraries, these elements could clearly apply to other libraries as well. This is where the need to understand the library's structure can benefit greatly from staff input. For example, the Library and Archives at the University of York in England used extensive and detailed feedback from staff to help restructure, while examining climate issues as well.[27] Andrews et al. identify several issues that have been unearthed from such a process:

> As the library moves toward peer-to-peer, flexible, and emergent approaches in dealing with users, it must do so internally as well, creating new organizational structures including: a more flat and flexible staff hierarchy; increased self-service and user-driven programs and processes; greater attention to professional development; succession planning; and new positions and job categories.[28]

They go on to state additional key findings:

> Service trends emerged, including: the need to examine public service desks with a critical eye toward consolidation for improved

service; students' desire for more self-service options, particularly the ability to reserve individual and group study spaces; and a need for technical assistance from the service desks.[29]

Similar patterns and trends can be found elsewhere. According to Meier and Miller, "At Penn State University Libraries, we are endeavoring to support a library and user community in a state of flux by moving from a culture of rigidity to one of flexibility . . . Key takeaways include encouraging a culture of experimentation, being open to failure, and keeping lines of communication open to strengthen collaboration."[30] One of the critical common elements in the literature and research is the increased emphasis on flexibility and adaptability. Andrews et al. state, "Be flexible and unafraid to fail."[31] This is one of the most solid takeaways when considering solutions for library organization and structure.

One way to approach this structurally so as to foster innovation appears to be flattening organizations. J. Stephen Town reports a flattened hierarchy that "was intended to reduce hierarchical transaction costs, and improve communication between staff and the senior team."[32] Yoose and Knight report a similar approach at the Grinnell College Libraries: "The outcome of this restructuring is the cluster organizational structure: a flat structure consisting of several work groups formed around library operations with shared leadership, including librarians and library staff."[33] No doubt some flattening of the hierarchy may be the result of cuts and redistributing workloads. Still, this flattening seems to be a common theme for libraries that seek to be innovative on an ongoing basis.

Another key element, according to Yoose and Knight, is staff involvement from the beginning: "Best practices for change management include staff buy-in at the beginning planning stages of the change, clear communication during the process, and transparency of the change process, including reasons and benefits of the change."[34] The benefits of widespread participation in the change process are well known. One interesting restructuring at UCT Libraries required new ways to share skills and information after reorganizing. This was done by engaging team leads. According to Raju et al., "It is the responsibility of the team leader to keep abreast of the growth within that particular service, and that would include conducting research and engaging with experts nationally and internationally."[35] When considering just how many changes and programs are being developed at large academic and public libraries, this seems to be a good way to allow information to spread.

Another solution in larger systems is piloting. At schools like Johnson & Wales University, which has four campuses in different states, libraries are often able to pilot ideas or programs that can then be ported over to other campuses if successful. Juntunen shares a similar approach used at three different Finnish universities, where "the campus libraries have maintained their tradition of creating and testing new services on their own. This has led to positive competition, where the most successful new ideas are taken in use within the whole library."[36]

At Penn State and other institutions, another approach has been to engage in what they refer to as "rapid prototyping." The philosophy behind this approach to finding solutions is to try things out even if all the bugs have not yet been worked out. According to Meier and Miller, "The speed of rapid prototyping is achieved by spending less time in the research and design phases and instead creating an initial version as fast as possible."[37] The only caveat seems to be that efforts in this regard need to be advertised as such.

Lastly, another approach of libraries looking to reorganize, and one similar to rapid prototyping, is to remember that libraries are essentially about learning and should embody that in their approach. Citing work by other researchers, Jantz notes "a strong learning orientation as a critical factor in the innovation implementation stage."[38]

J. STEPHEN TOWN'S RESTRUCTURING ITEM LIST

- Customer focus: excellent service
- Scholarship: add value to research, teaching, learning
- Vision, inspiration and empowerment: dynamic, flexible, forward-thinking
- Respect, honesty, and transparency: communicate openly

SOURCE: J. Stephen Town, "Evidence-Based Organizational Change: People Surveys, Strategies, and Structures," *Library Management* 36, no. 8/9 (2015): 634.

Civility and Ethics

Any discussion of library planning should incorporate a consideration of civility and ethics. One approach has been to explore cultures and structures that promote and support what is referred to as good citizenship. According to Bolino and Turnley, "Good citizenship is thought to include a variety of employee behaviors, such as taking on additional assignments, voluntarily assisting other people at work, keeping up with developments in one's field or profession, following company rules even when no one is looking, promoting and protecting the organization, and keeping a positive attitude and tolerating inconveniences at work."[39] According to Patricia Katopol, "good organizational citizenship exhibits behaviors along five dimensions": assisting coworkers, courtesy, sportsmanship, conscientiousness, and civic virtue.[40] In their discussion of good citizenship, Bolino and Turnley note: "In some recent empirical studies . . . several researchers investigating firm performance in a variety of industries have found that employee citizenship does produce tangible benefits for organizations."[41] This points to an intermingling between structure and culture that is important to consider.

One way that good citizenship can be fostered is by codifying and embedding these elements into standard performance reviews. According to Chris Bart, "The final leg of the journey on the road to an ethical work environment . . . involves adjusting the organization's performance management system to include ethical behaviour as an important criterion for performance measurement, promotion, and possibly even termination. This is the acid test that determines just how seriously a company takes its own ethics/values code."[42]

Another way is by making sure, as noted above, that everyone has a chance to participate in planning. According to Andrews, "Every person in every department knows that his or her ideas and opinions are valued, and that he or she has real input into the library's day-to-day operation; staff are encouraged and rewarded for bringing forth new ideas that improve service."[43]

Another way that good citizenship can be supported is by paying attention to employees' work-life balance. According to Bolino and Turnley, "In one study, for example, employees were more willing to go beyond the call of duty when they worked for companies that offered support which enabled them to more easily balance their work and family responsibilities, assisted them

---

TIPS ON CIVILITY

- Pay attention
- Listen
- Speak kindly
- Assume the best
- Respect others' opinions
- Respect other people's time and space
- Be inclusive
- Acknowledge others
- Accept and give praise
- Apologize earnestly
- Assert yourself
- Take responsibility
- Accept and give constructive criticism
- Refrain from idle complaints
- Be a considerate guest

SOURCE: Choose Civility, "About Choose Civility," http://choosecivility.org/about/.

through difficult times, provided them with benefits they could not afford, and helped their children do things they would not have been able to do otherwise."[44] Moreover, an organization that pays attention to the needs of its staff will almost certainly be one that pays attention to the needs of its customers, or in our case, patrons.

Libraries should also foster a culture of caring. This is accomplished only when the management truly cares about staff. Bolino and Turnley state, for example: "Managers who demonstrate loyalty and show professional respect for their employees are also likely to elicit higher levels of citizenship. Conversely, employees who see their supervisors as rather distant, or feel ignored by them, are typically less likely to engage in citizenship behavior."[45] This assertion is, therefore, both a solution and a warning at the same time. Hand-in-hand with caring is leading by example, another important thing for all library leaders to do. Again, according to Bolino and Turnley, "Managers who expect their employees to go above and beyond the call of duty, then, have to be willing to do so themselves. For example, the CEO of JetBlue, David Neeleman, frequently loads bags or serves customers himself in order to convey that all employees are expected to pitch in where necessary."[46] It is important to stand side by side with the staff who are doing the work.

Library managers often have to make difficult decisions in a variety of spheres that pertain to staff, allocation of limited resources, and other areas. The library should be structured so that these decisions are as transparent as possible. Again, this can be challenging when staff are dedicated to their main area or service point in the library. Pixey Mosley notes: "Because individuals are looking for support for their specific areas and may be passionately committed to a particular position, when a leader has to make the decision in favor of one view over another, someone will not be happy. Making the decision based on a transparent process that allows for open dialogue can help diffuse the emotions of the situation, but a certain amount of win/lose dynamic is unavoidable."[47] She goes on to state:

> There are several benefits to explaining one's decision-making process, even if one cannot share every detail. Acknowledging that a decision was difficult and complex and speaking to the various factors that had to be weighed in the decision creates an opportunity to develop future leaders. It also helps diffuse some of the personalized resentment of the decision and demonstrates that the decision was not about the individual but incorporated the data and strategic context. Finally, it makes the administrator seem more

human and engaged with employees rather than seeming distant, on a pedestal, or only engaged with institutional administrators or selected individuals.[48]

Lastly, an environment that encourages people to own up to their mistakes is one that will thrive. If individuals cannot admit to errors, they will not learn from them. More critically, as a manager, if mistakes are not admitted, the support and confidence of the staff erode. Mosley notes further that a leader "must be willing to be human and openly admit to having made a mistake with ethical ramifications."[49] This is not always easy to do, but it is necessary.

Conclusion

Libraries are faced with many challenges, from the rapidly changing external environment to the need to stretch budgets further and further. Patrons' needs are changing as well, which requires new and more open ways of thinking. Exploring changes in organizational structure through concepts such as flattening, piloting, and prototyping helps to meet these challenges. Finally, fostering good citizenship in the work environment has a positive impact on staff, and in turn the customers that libraries serve.

QUESTIONS FOR DISCUSSION

- How is your library organized?
- If you could reorganize your library from scratch, what might that look like?
- How have your users' needs changed in recent years?
- How are you exploring users' needs in your library?
- What processes do you have in place to foster innovation in your library?
- How supportive is your library's structure and culture for supporting work-life balance?

NOTES

1. Reggie Raju et al., "Restructuring for Relevance: A Paradigm Shift for Academic Libraries," *Library Management* 39, no. 6-7 (2018): 419.
2. Raju et al., "Restructuring for Relevance," 423.
3. Mohsen Nazarzadeh Zare et al., "From Change to Organizational Transformation: A Survey of Tehran Medical Science University's Libraries," *Library Management* 36, no. 1/2 (2015): 158.
4. Ronald C. Jantz, "The Determinants of Organizational Innovation: An Interpretation and Implications for Research Libraries," *College & Research Libraries* 76, no. 4 (May 2015): 515.
5. Jantz, "The Determinants of Organizational Innovation," 516.
6. Lisa Moniz, interview, April 29, 2019.
7. Diane L. Velasquez, "Impact of Technology on Organizational Change in Public Libraries: A Qualitative Study," in *Advances in Library Administration and Organization* (Bingley, UK: Emerald Group, 2010), 161.
8. J. Stephen Town, "Evidence-Based Organizational Change: People Surveys, Strategies, and Structures," *Library Management* 36, no. 8/9 (2015): 633.
9. Camille Andrews et al., "'From 'Library as Place' to 'Library as Platform': Redesigning the 21st Century Academic Library," in *The Future of Library Space* (Bingley, UK: Emerald Group, 2016), 161.
10. Town, "Evidence-Based Organizational Change," 623.
11. Andrews et al., "'From 'Library as Place' to 'Library as Platform,'" 146.
12. Jantz, "The Determinants of Organizational Innovation," 512.
13. Anne Ford, "When Universities Cut, Libraries Bleed: How Academic Libraries Respond to Shrinking Offerings," *American Libraries* 49, no. 11/12 (November 2018): 18.
14. Beverly Goldberg, "Are Harvard's Realignment Throes Unique—or a Cautionary Tale?" *American Libraries* 43, no. 5/6 (May 2012): 26.
15. Goldberg, "Are Harvard's Realignment Throes Unique," 27.
16. Raju et al., "Restructuring for Relevance," 424.
17. Ford, "When Universities Cut, Libraries Bleed," 18.
18. Ford, "When Universities Cut, Libraries Bleed," 18.
19. Pixey Mosley, "Engaging Leadership," *Library Leadership & Management* 28, no. 1 (January 2014): 1.
20. Mosley, "Engaging Leadership," 3.
21. Joanna Bryant, "What Are Students Doing in Our Library? Ethnography as a Method of Exploring Library User Behaviour," *Library and Information Research* 33, no. 103 (2009): 8.
22. Andrews et al., "'From 'Library as Place' to 'Library as Platform,'" 164.
23. Bruce L. Keisling and Claudene Sproles, "Reviewing and Reforming Library Service Points: Lessons in Review and Planning Services, Building Layout, and Organizational Culture," *Library Management* 38, no. 8/9 (2017): 428.
24. Mark E. de Jong, "Service Design for Libraries: An Introduction," in *Advances in Librarianship* (Bingley, UK: Emerald Group, 2014), 137–51.

25. Arja Juntunen et al., "Reinventing the Academic Library and Its Mission: Service Design in Three Merged Finnish Libraries," in *Mergers and Alliances: The Wider View* (Bingley, UK: Emerald Group, 2015), 225–46, esp. 235.

26. Andrews et al., "'From 'Library as Place' to 'Library as Platform,''" 149.

27. Town, "Evidence-Based Organizational Change," 625.

28. Andrews et al., "'From 'Library as Place' to 'Library as Platform,''" 147.

29. Andrews et al., "'From 'Library as Place' to 'Library as Platform,''" 161.

30. John J. Meier and Rebecca K. Miller, "Fail Early and Often to Succeed: A Case for Rapid Prototyping in Libraries," *Library Leadership & Management* 33, no. 1 (October 2018): 1.

31. Andrews et al., "'From 'Library as Place' to 'Library as Platform,''" 166.

32. Town, "Evidence-Based Organizational Change," 635.

33. Becky Yoose and Cecilia Knight, "Clusters: A Study of a Non-Traditional Academic Library Organizational Model," *Library Leadership & Management* 30, no. 3 (January 2016): 1.

34. Yoose and Knight, "Clusters," 4.

35. Raju et al., "Restructuring for Relevance," 427.

36. Juntunen et al., "Reinventing the Academic Library and Its Mission," 234.

37. Meier and Miller, "Fail Early and Often to Succeed," 3.

38. Jantz, "The Determinants of Organizational Innovation," 516.

39. Mark C. Bolino and William H. Turnley, "Going the Extra Mile: Cultivating and Managing Employee Citizenship Behavior," *Academy of Management Executive* 17, no. 3 (August 2003): 60.

40. Patricia Katopol, "Employees Who Do More—Organizational Citizenship Behavior," *Library Leadership & Management* 28, no. 4 (September 2014): 2–3.

41. Bolino and Turnley, "Going the Extra Mile," 61.

42. Chris Bart, "Ethics: The Key to Organizational Culture," *Canadian Manager* 36, no. 3 (fall 2011): 6.

43. Andrews et al., "'From 'Library as Place' to 'Library as Platform,''" 162.

44. Bolino and Turnley, "Going the Extra Mile," 62.

45. Bolino and Turnley, "Going the Extra Mile," 62.

46. Bolino and Turnley, "Going the Extra Mile," 67.

47. Mosley, "Engaging Leadership," 2.

48. Mosley, "Engaging Leadership," 3.

49. Mosley, "Engaging Leadership," 7.

17

Develop a Trusting
Work Environment

Employee trust is an essential part of a dynamic, productive organization. Barbara Fredrickson, a psychology professor at the University of North Carolina, has studied the impact of positive emotions, including trust. "Positive emotions . . . trigger broadened, curious, and optimistic patterns of thought together with more spontaneous and energetic behavior" and have been shown to improve job performance, worker health, and productivity levels.[1] These emotions also lead to individuals widening their field of trust and identifying other groups as "us" rather than as "them."[2] The reflections of eighteen academic library deans and directors point to the importance of trust in library organizations. Collectively they view trust as "mutual trust with their supervisors, trust in (and among) their leadership team, and trust in their colleagues in working with other campus units. When trust is present in all three of these areas, directors seem to act with confidence and to empower their organization far more so than when it is partially or entirely absent."[3] Trust in the library workplace is also rooted in psychological safety, or workers' perception of how safe it is to take risks at work and express their ideas and feelings.

Trust between an individual and the organization and its leaders leads to greater group participation, sharing, and learning.[4] This chapter will explore how an organization can promote trust through its psychological contract with workers, as well as through leaders' interactions, employees' voice and engagement, and employees' growth.

Psychological Contract

A psychological contract between an employee and employer is an unwritten set of rules or expectations that come along with the job—it is what an employee gives to an organization in return for what he or she may get from it. An employer may expect "competence, effort, compliance, commitment, and loyalty" and an employee may expect in return fair and consistent treatment, advancement and skill development opportunities, and job security.[5] (See figure 17.1.) This employee-organization relationship (EOR) can be an important predictor of employee trust.[6]

Balancing the EOR in an ever-changing environment is the challenge of managers and organizational leaders. As work requirements change, leaders must communicate new expectations to their employees.[7] In libraries, this may involve a new outreach initiative or a project collaboration with an academic division that did not exist when the librarian was hired. If a balanced psychological contract can be maintained, employees will have a higher level of trust in the workplace. Once this trust is established, organizations will see more positive behaviors, commitment, loyalty, knowledge-sharing, and innovation from their workers.[8] However, if the employee thinks that the organization is not delivering its contribution to the EOR for whatever reason, a breach of the psychological contract can result. As Ronald Sims says, "the violation of the psychological contract can signal to the participants that the parties no longer share (or never shared) a common set of values or goals."[9] The perception of contract breach may occur when the organization's promises fall short or are not delivered, and depending on the "specific inducement under consideration (e.g., pay vs. recognition)," the employees' reactions may involve disappointment, frustration, or even resentment. Moreover, contract breaches related to work experiences (rather than work expectations) typically elicit stronger negative reactions from employees.[10] Research shows that contract breaches have a "strong negative effect on job satisfaction" and increase burnout, cynicism, emotional exhaustion, and "a lower sense of personal accomplishment."[11]

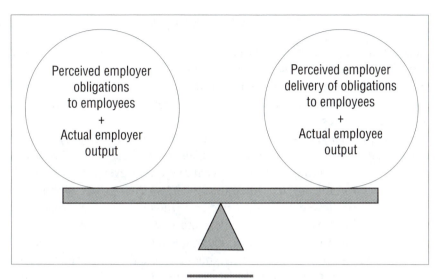

FIGURE 17.1
A Balanced Psychological Contract

Libraries can foster a more trusting and committed workforce by maintaining a balanced EOR. This can be accomplished in several ways. First, hiring teams should clarify the library's expectations of the position during the recruitment process. Second, as expectations change and libraries shift in their needs and goals, updated expectations should be communicated and new training initiatives implemented.[12] Next, policies and decisions as they relate to changes in work expectations should be clearly relayed to workers. Finally, libraries should promote "consensus and cooperation rather than control and coercion" in order to develop positive psychological contracts and in turn cultivate trust with their employees.[13]

EOR CHECKLIST

- Are employees treated fairly and equitably?
- Do employees feel a sense of job security?
- Is training provided when policies change, or a new initiative is implemented?
- Are employees' career expectations being met?
- Do employees have opportunities to develop their skills?
- Are employees involved, and do they have influence in the workplace?
- Does management keep its promises?

Leader Interactions

Leaders' interactions with their employees can also promote trust in the organization: first is the leader's perception of his or her power and how that power is used; second is the role of the leader in creating a psychologically safe work environment; and third is the importance of humility in leaders as it relates to trust.

When a manager asserts his or her power over an employee in an adversarial or authoritarian way, trust is difficult to establish. Power has been defined as "getting others to do what one wants, even if they resist."[14] Several studies indicate that when managers use their power in this way, it is "fixed" or viewed as competitive and leads to employee frustration and stress.[15] To create a more trusting and effective dynamic, managers should share their power. Empowering employees to take control and act on their own not only increases trust, but also actually enhances the leader's power. A study of positive library leaders indicates that empowering employees is not only a top-ranking past trait, but is also anticipated as an important future trait as part of putting people first.[16] To instill trust, successful library leaders should approach their relationships in a collaborative way rather than being adversarial.[17]

Using Student Workers to Help Create a Kind and Safe Workplace

VALERIE FREEMAN
Johnson & Wales University Library Charlotte, North Carolina

Our library is somewhat unique in its staffing, since it relies heavily on Federal Work-Study students and a single student assistant. When I took over supervision of this pool of employees, I think everyone saw them more as students than as employees, and to be sure, that was a large part of their identity. But I also saw an opportunity to strengthen their work experience. Furthermore, these work-study students are the ones whom visitors see first when they come into the library, and as such, I found it important to spend time not only on their basic training—which covered checking out items and shelving—but also on those soft skills that are transferable to any field. These soft skills, which include communication and building relationships, are central to building a trusting and safe workplace for workers at all levels.

The training of these work-study students has taken many iterations over the years, beginning with focusing on the work and the processes involved, and evolving from there based on the students' perceived needs, wherever I felt that gaps existed. Now, in training at the beginning of the year, we go through the details of handling the circulation processes and other details of their responsibilities, such as shelving and displays. But the majority of our time in that training session is spent on safety and security training, as well as customer service training. I bring in a security officer from our security department to share our university's policy and best practices in dealing with certain events. An additional focus is on customer service training, since that will be important in most fields that the students eventually enter. We also spend significant time discussing how to best impact the students and other patrons who enter our library.

Another element that I have brought to their supervision is getting to know them through conversation. This helps them become more comfortable in their workspace and when interacting with librarians. In turn, this facilitates a better service model with our patrons, making for more satisfied customers even when we cannot satisfy every desire. The student workers become an integrated part of the library workflow, and because they feel a part of it, they bring their relationship-building skills to the fore when dealing with patrons. It is the personal touch that will bring people into the library. The library relies heavily on the student workers in their various roles and they know it, which makes them feel valued, which they in turn convey to the patrons.

The result of this effort, on all levels, is that the library is a welcoming place on campus where students assemble and gather to work, socialize, and hang out. The student employees are often deeply engaged in their work. Students who come in asking for help just as often ask them for assistance as they do the librarians, which helps keep the student workers engaged and motivated, as well as helping to ensure that the library meets the needs of the campus in as many ways as possible.

Organizational leaders can also build trust through psychological safety, that is, the understanding that there will be no punishment for "mistakes, speaking your mind, [or] creativity."[18] Amy Edmundson, a professor at the Harvard Business School, has found in her research that trust is a foundational element of the psychological safety of an organizational team.[19] Paul Santagata, the head of industry at Google, surveyed Google employees and found psychological safety to be the most critical success factor among five commonalities of teams.[20] Santagata suggests that leaders replace blame with curiosity and ask for feedback on their message delivery to employees if they would like to increase trust. Leaders can also work on opening lines of communication so that all voices can be heard; promote the sharing of ideas; and encourage active listening at all levels of the organization.

SANTAGATA'S "JUST LIKE ME" LEADER REFLECTION

- This person has beliefs, perspectives, and opinions, just like me.
- This person has hopes, anxieties, and vulnerabilities, just like me.
- This person has friends, family, and perhaps children who love them, just like me.
- This person wants to feel respected, appreciated, and competent, just like me.
- This person wishes for peace, joy, and happiness, just like me.

SOURCE: Laura Delizonna, "High-Performing Teams Need Psychological Safety: Here's How to Create It," *Harvard Business Review,* last updated August 24, 2017, https://hbr.org/2017/08/high-performing-teams-need-psychological-safety-heres-how-to-create-it.

Lastly, leaders can strive for humility. "Those who have humility are more likely to appreciate the contributions of others without feeling threatened by them."[21] This begins with leaders knowing themselves and feeling secure with who they are as individuals. Leaders understand when they have knowledge, but should admit when it is lacking. This means "they do not pretend to know something that they do not know in practice."[22] Again, this allows the workers to grow in a trusting environment without fear of offending the leader. Studies indicate that humble leaders evoke employees' loyalty, creativity, satisfaction, loyalty, mutual respect, and *trust.*[23]

Employee Voice and Engagement

Along with leaders, organizations should support employees having a voice, so that their opinions, ideas, and concerns can be shared without reprisal. The degree to which this is allowed by the organization has an impact on employee engagement. The greater the opportunity for employees to have a voice, the higher their level of engagement. Employee voice has also been linked to increased motivation and creativity at work.[24] Thus, libraries that allow employees a voice will have a more positive and engaged library workforce.

Both trust and voice are positively linked to the employees' relationship with both their immediate manager and the higher administration. However, organizational *engagement* is more strongly linked to higher administration than direct managers in an organization where the employee has a voice and feels safe using it. If employees are heard at the higher levels in library organizations, they will feel more satisfied and committed.[25] Libraries can encourage employee voice in a number of ways. First, they need to provide opportunities for the higher administration to hear the views of lower-level staff. Second, direct managers should facilitate employees' participation by relaying their views to administrators and acknowledging that they have been heard. These exchange opportunities can occur both in-person and through collective responses, teams, or surveys. Additionally, both direct managers and the upper administration should follow up on employees' ideas and input. Being heard and then dismissed does not develop organizational trust. The use of attitude surveys or suggestion schemes are also ways to collect information on employees' ideas and concerns.[26] Finally, library organizations should find ways to recognize the ideas, as well as the efforts, of their employees.

WAYS TO GATHER IDEAS

- Schedule regular staff meetings to share ideas.
- Promote idea creation on shared online forms.
- Hold brainstorming meetings to generate new ideas.
- Develop ways for the staff to offer suggestions.
- Provide collaborative spaces for projects and idea-sharing.
- Offer an open door for idea discussions.

Employee Growth

As part of facilitating trust through the psychological contract with employees, organizations should also try to provide opportunities for staff development. In a dysfunctional environment, leaders sometimes wield their power to limit or deny educational opportunities for staff, which breaks the trust relationship. The goal should be to move in the opposite direction. "Education and Continuous Learning is one of the five key action areas adopted by the American Library Association to fulfill its mission of promoting the highest quality library and information services for all people."[27] Professional development opportunities can be online, in-house, remote, or external.

Libraries are deeply engaged in continuing education through online webinars, e-courses, workshops, and conferences, many of which are free. Such learning opportunities are extensive, and the ALA's Office for Human Resource Development and Recruitment offers an "Education and Continuing Professional Development" list which is a good starting point (at www.ala.org/aboutala/offices/hrdr/educprofdev/educationcontinuous). For organizations with an adequate budget, funds should be set aside for continual learning opportunities. Other ideas include quarterly meetings with indirect reports, creating meaningful training programs, and adding teams into the organizational structure.[28]

Special projects or assignments provide other chances for library staff growth. Research suggests that encouraging this kind of skill development and having employees take on problems to solve helps create a trusting work environment.[29] William Kahn notes the importance of meaningful work tasks: "Meaningful tasks demanded both routine and new skills, allowing people to experience a sense of both competence . . . and growth and learning."[30]

Leo Appleton offers several other suggestions for developing the skills of librarians. He employs "strategic staff development" in which library staff are trained in the skill areas they need in order to move up to the next organizational level. In addition to workshops and conferences, utilizing formal study programs (such as information technology), job shadowing, mentoring, and reading groups can be helpful. (Reading groups gather to read and discuss current library literature and issues.)[31] At Utah State University's Merrill-Cazier Library, the use of staff development committees has also seen success.[32] All of these ideas promote staff development and encourage employees' trust in their library organizations.

Conclusion

Developing trust in the library organization leads to engaged and productive employees and leaders who are more empowered and confident. While developing trust can be a challenging task for organizations, it is possible. Striving for a balanced psychological contract with library employees is one area. Promoting humble leaders who empower employees also plays a role. Encouraging employees' voice in a safe environment promotes both engagement and trust. Finally, supporting continuing education and internal training opportunities contributes to building a trusting library workplace.

QUESTIONS FOR REFLECTION

- Does the library organization have a balanced employee-organization relationship?
- How is the library organization establishing employee trust?
- What ways can my organization encourage employees' voice?
- How does the library organization provide opportunities for employee growth and development?

NOTES

1. Barbara L. Fredrickson, "Positive Emotions Broaden and Build," in *Advances in Experimental Social Psychology*, ed. E. A. Plant and P. G. Devine, vol. 47 (Amsterdam: Elsevier, 2013), 34–35.
2. Fredrickson, "Positive Emotions Broaden and Build," 23.
3. Roger C. Schonfeld, "Organizing the Work of the Research Library," ITHAKA S+R, August 18, 2016, https://sr.ithaka.org/wp-content/uploads/2016/08/SR_Report _Organizing_Work_Research_Library_081816.pdf.
4. Wenxing Liu et al., "Abusive Supervisors and Employee Creativity: The Mediating Role of Psychological Safety and Organizational Intent," *Management Decision* 54, no. 1 (2016): 134.
5. Michael Armstrong, *A Handbook of Human Resource Management Practice,* 10th ed. (Philadelphia: Kogan Page, 2003), 279.
6. Ming-Chuan Yu, Qiang Mai, Sang-Bing Tsai, and Yi Dai, "An Empirical Study on Organizational Trust, Employee-Organization Relationship, and Innovative Behavior from the Integrated Perspective of Social Exchange and Organizational Sustainability," *Sustainability* 10, no. 3 (2018): 864.
7. Armstrong, *A Handbook of Human Resource Management Practice*, 281.
8. Yu et al., "An Empirical Study," 864–65.
9. Ronald R. Sims, "Human Resource Management's Role in Clarifying the New Psychological Contract," *Human Resource Management* 33, no. 3 (fall 1994): 375.
10. Lisa Shurer Lambert, Jeffrey R. Edwards, and Daniel M. Cable, "Breach and Fulfillment of the Psychological Contract: A Comparison of Traditional and Expanded Views," *Personal Psychology* 56 (2003): 896.

11. Hakan Erkutlu and Jamel Chafra, "Benevolent Leadership and Psychological Well-Being," *Leadership & Organization Development Journal* 37, no. 3 (2016).

12. Sims, "Human Resource Management's Role," 379–80.

13. Michael Armstrong, *Armstrong's Handbook of Management and Leadership: Developing Effective People Skills for Better Leadership and Management* (Philadelphia: Kogan Page, 2012), 181.

14. Dean Tjosvold and Haifa Sun, "Effects of Power Concepts and Employee Performance on Managers' Empowering," *Leadership & Organization Development Journal* 27, no. 3 (2006): 218.

15. Tjosvold and Sun, "Effects of Power Concepts," 218.

16. Jason Martin, "What Do Academic Librarians Value in a Leader? Reflections on Past Positive Library Leaders and a Consideration of Future Library Leaders," *College & Research Library News* 79, no. 6 (2018).

17. Laura Delizonna, "High-Performing Teams Need Psychological Safety: Here's How to Create It," *Harvard Business Review*, August 24, 2017, https://hbr.org/2017/08/high-performing-teams-need-psychological-safety-heres-how-to-create-it.

18. Delizonna, "High-Performing Teams Need Psychological Safety."

19. Amy Edmondson, "Psychological Safety and Learning Behavior in Work Teams," *Administrative Science Quarterly* 44, no. 2 (June 1999): 375.

20. Julia Rozovsky, "The Five Keys to a Successful Google Team," *re:Work*, last updated November 17, 2015, https://rework.withgoogle.com/blog/five-keys-to-a-successful-google-team/.

21. Lurdes Goncalves and Filipa Brandao, "The Relation between Leader's Humility and Team Creativity," *International Journal of Organizational Analysis* 25, no. 4 (2017): 689.

22. Goncalves and Brandao, "The Relation between Leader's Humility and Team Creativity," 689.

23. Goncalves and Brandao, "The Relation between Leader's Humility and Team Creativity"; Bradley P. Owns and David R. Hekman, "Modeling How to Grow: An Inductive Examination of Humble Leader Behaviors, Contingencies, and Outcomes," *Academy of Management Journal* 55, no. 4 (2012): 787–818.

24. Asadollah Ganjali and Saeed Rezaee, "Linking Perceived Employee Voice and Creativity," *Iranian Journal of Management Studies* 9, no. 1 (2016): 186.

25. Chris Rees, Kerstin Alfes, and Mark Gatenby, "Employee Voice and Engagement: Connections and Consequences," *International Journal of Human Resource Management* 24, no. 14: 2791.

26. Armstrong, *Handbook of Human Resource Management Practice.*

27. American Library Association, "Education and Continuous Learning," April 19, 2007, http://www.ala.org/aboutala/missionhistory/keyactionareas/education action/educationcontinuing.

28. Schonfeld, "Organizing the Work of the Research Library."

29. Douglas R. May, Richard L. Gilson, and Lynn M. Harter, "The Psychological Conditions of Meaningfulness, Safety, and Availability and the Engagement of the Human Spirit at Work," *Journal of Occupational and Organizational Psychology* 77 (2004): 33.

30. William A. Kahn, "Psychological Conditions of Personal Engagement and Disengagement at Work," *Academy of Management Journal* 33, no 4 (December 1990): 704.

31. Leo Appleton, "Training and Development for Librarians: Why Bother?" Elsevier Library Connect, last updated August 21, 2018, https://libraryconnect.elsevier.com/articles/training-and-development-librarians-why-bother.

32. Erin L. Davis and Kacy Lundstrom, "Creating Effective Staff Development Committees: A Case Study," Library Faculty & Staff Publications, Paper 107, 2011, https://digitalcommons.usu.edu/cgi/viewcontent.cgi?referer=https://www.google.com/&httpsredir=1&article=1106&context=lib_pubs.

18

Organizational Training

ncivility and dysfunction must be addressed at all levels, from individual workers to managers to the upper administration. Most importantly, the library organization as a whole must push for improvements on multiple fronts over an extended period of time in order to see real improvements in the dynamics of a library workplace. One-time training sessions are ineffective. Combating incivility and dysfunction should become a part of the organization's ongoing training program. This chapter will briefly highlight five major training areas that library organizations can utilize: bias training, empathy training, microaggression awareness training, conflict management training, and diversity training.

Bias Training

Biases are defined as "attitudes or stereotypes that affect our understanding, actions, and decisions in an unconscious manner."[1] Of the 150 different kinds of cognitive bias, five impact the workplace. The first is affinity bias, or our natural gravitation toward people who look like us. The second is the halo effect, in which our positive impression about someone influences how we evaluate his or her character. The third is perception bias, which involves our stereotyping and making assumptions about certain groups, while mistakenly thinking we are making impartial judgments. (This is related to implicit bias, in which we unconsciously attribute particular qualities to a member of a certain social group.) The fourth is confirmation bias, in which people search for, interpret, or accept information that tends to confirm their previously existing beliefs and conceptions. Finally, groupthink is when an individual loses some identity when trying to become part of a group through imitation and refrains from offering his or her opinions.[2]

Bias can negatively impact libraries in many ways. It may lead to discriminatory hiring practices and fail to promote diversity in the library staff. It may also impact interpersonal exchanges in the library workplace, as well as productivity when library staffs are drained of "emotional and mental energy . . . to cope with chronic implicit bias."[3] Bias can impact organizational culture, performance appraisals, promotions, and leader development.[4] It can also limit the formation of trust in the library, which is an important factor in a positive workplace. The Association of College & Research Libraries reports that workers with "implicit bias have more difficulty forming trusting relationships," and one of the steps to counter bias is for libraries to promote training in "cultural competency."[5]

Library organizations should encourage individuals to explore and become aware of their personal biases. Project Implicit offers a free "Implicit Association Test" for all biases at www.implicit.harvard.edu. The Oklahoma City Human Resources Society offers six steps for changing bias through training: (1) reflect on current biases, (2) confront the reasons for biases, (3) use conversation to debunk biases, (4) understand

---

CHARACTERISTICS OF BIASES

- They are not necessarily aligned with conscious beliefs.
- They have real-world effects.
- They are unconscious.
- They are pervasive.
- They are malleable.

SOURCE: Cheryl Staats, Kelly Capatosto, Lena Tenney, and Sarah Mamo, "State of the Science: Implicit Bias Review," Kirwan Institute, Ohio State University, 2017 Edition: 10, http://kirwaninstitute.osu.edu/implicit-bias-training/resources/2017-implicit-bias-review.pdf.

individuals for who they are, (5) connect with diverse people, and (6) discuss attempts to overcome biases.[6]

There are a number of options for organizations to approach bias training. Some research has pointed to the success of negation training, in which participants choose a meaningful "that's wrong!" response option when they view bias in a picture-word association.[7] Another approach is motivation awareness; that is, awareness of one's intention when acting. As personal motivation is linked to implicit bias, this bias can be reduced by increasing one's awareness that "behavior displays their moral intentions and values."[8] Finally, increasing mindfulness through meditation has also been linked to reducing bias.

Empathy Training

According to Zahavi, empathy is "an intentionality directed towards the other's experience."[9] Empathy requires the ability to "show unconditional positive regard, listen accurately, and be able to take the perspective of others."[10] There are three components to empathy: cognitive (seeing the other's perspective), affective (experiencing the other's feelings), and behavioral (communicating understanding of another's experience).[11] Katelyn Angell, in "Applications of Edith Stein's Empathy Theory to Library Science," reflects how empathy "has the potential to enhance library service."[12] As stated in *Library Worklife*'s article on empathy, "As you become more adept at understanding your own feelings, you'll get better at understanding the feelings of the people around you."[13] This can apply to library workplace dynamics as well.

A variety of empathy training methods has been used, which include a mix of experiential training, didactic instruction, skill training, mindfulness, video stimuli, and writing exercises.[14] Experiential training involves facilitators leading learners through experiences. In 1984 David Kolb devised a well-known model in this area that he called the Reflective Learning Cycle. This lecture-free method involves reflection, the formulation of guiding principles, applying learning, and receiving feedback.[15] In a review of twenty-nine studies across several professions (including education and social work), experiential methods combined with didactic communication (instructor-led content delivery) were the most popular ones for empathy training.[16] Also popular was a combination of didactic communication and skills training (e.g., communication or interpersonal skills). Both of these combined methods produced positive results more than 90 percent of the time in the case studies.[17] The use of video along with written empathetic responses to a scene is another possible method for empathy training. Finally, as with bias training, mindfulness can also assist with empathy training, since it leads to compassion for others. Shauna Shapiro has done much work in the area of mindfulness and compassion; see her TEDx Talk "The Power of Mindfulness: What You Practice Grows Stronger."

Another approach to empathy training which includes a writing exercise has been suggested by Magnus Englander, a professor at Malmö University in Sweden. This approach involves three steps—understanding, reflection, and verbalized empathy. This approach involves writing a ten-minute reflection and sharing it with a group, and then repeating the process with new insight.[18]

IDEAS FOR INCREASING EMPATHY

The Center for Building a Culture of Empathy and Compassion's "Empathy Training Manual" incorporates a number of different training plans in the areas of self-empathy, accepting others, accurate listening, and perspective taking. You can find the manual at http://cultureofempathy.com/Referenes/Experts/Others/FilesMarieke-Kingma-Empathy-Training-Manual.pdf.

Microaggression Awareness Training

Microaggressions are defined as "brief and commonplace daily verbal, behavioral, and environmental indignities, whether intentional or unintentional, that communicate hostile, derogatory, or negative racial, gender, sexual-orientation, or religious slights and insults to the target person or group."[19] They can be divided into three forms: microassault, microinsult, and microinvalidation. Microassaults are either verbal or nonverbal derogatory attacks that may include "name-calling, avoidant behavior, or purposeful discriminatory actions."[20] Microinsults are subtle, rude communications which are demeaning and "represent subtle snubs . . . and hidden insulting message[s]."[21] Finally, microinvalidations are communications that negate the "feelings, or experiential reality" of the person.[22]

In libraries, much recent attention has been given to the topic through workshops and presentations that share LIS Microaggressions zine stories (www.lismicroaggressions.com) in the areas of race, nationality, status, sex, age, religion, politics, health, and marital status.[23] Other examples include Nicole Cooke's analysis of her first-year experiences, including microaggressions, as a woman of color in academic libraries, and Jaena Alabi's research, which found a higher frequency of microaggressions targeting academic librarians of color.[24]

Training programs in microaggression involve inquiry and self-exploration as the first step by exploring the question "What does it mean to be (fill in minority)?" Awareness training in this area includes the ability to identify microaggressions, understand their impact, and take corrective actions for one's personal biases.[25] The exploration and understanding of both bias and diversity are key to these training programs.

STRATEGIES FOR MICRORESISTANCE

1. Say something on the spot, so the aggressor knows your feeling of discomfort, disrespect, or hurt.

2. Say something to the aggressor privately in their office (or other appropriate location) at a time after the meeting or event where the incident occurred.

3. Open an ongoing dialogue to communicate your feelings and educate the aggressor.

4. Disengage somewhat from the aggressor by redirecting the conversation (i.e., change the subject) in order to avoid an emotional response that might escalate the exchange.

5. Engage in a proactive, nonreactive strategy called "microresistance."

SOURCE: Ronald A. Berk, "Microaggressions Trilogy Part 2: Microaggressions in the Academic Workplace," *New Forums Press* 31, no. 2 (May 2017): 76.

Conflict Management Training

While chapter 2 addressed handling conflict from the perspective of an individual library worker, and chapter 12 addressed handling conflict from a library leader's perspective, this section will introduce some methods for organizational training to reduce workplace conflict. In 2000, Edwards and Walton wrote about conflict in the academic library and the need for conflict resolution. They stated that "LIS could benefit from deeper study of how they are actually handling conflict."[26] While some progress has been made in the last two decades, in a 2018 study by the authors, 58 percent of library staffers are still not provided with conflict management training.[27]

To address specific issues of conflict in an organization, a third party is typically contracted. This type of conflict resolution typically involves assessment, identifying challenges, addressing the issues, and then reaching an agreement or resolution. Assessment is the first step and can be done by talking to a few "key stakeholders," or by more in-depth methods which involve many in-person interviews.[28] Initially, information should be gathered and stakeholders interviewed. (See the sidebar for these steps.). Once this is complete, an analysis of the information that has been gathered is undertaken. In this phase, findings are summarized, areas of agreement and disagreement are determined, and the potential for resolution is evaluated.[29] The steps to reach a resolution are then laid out and implemented. Lastly, the organization and stakeholders are given a final report of the entire process and its concluding agreements.[30]

INFORMATION-GATHERING STEPS IN CONFLICT RESOLUTION

1. Collect background information on stakeholders and pertinent documentation on the conflict's history and issues.
2. Identify stakeholders to interview (primary and secondary).
3. Call the interviewees.
4. Prepare interview questions (conflict history, importance, concerns, etc.).
5. Arrange and conduct the interviews.

SOURCE: Lawrence Susskind, Sarah McKeaman, and Jennifer Thomas-Larmer, *The Consensus Building Handbook: A Comprehensive Guide to Reaching Agreement* (Thousand Oaks, CA: Sage, 1999), 107.

Organizations can also implement more generic conflict management workshops that employ conflict management facilitators. The workshop curriculum includes practice for active listening, proper dialogue (such as the use of active verbs), and constructive confrontation. Events are recreated through role-playing or video analysis so that attendees can not only understand how to act and react to conflict situations, but also see this in action.[31] This type of interactive workshop can be delivered over one day, in small groups, or in a one-on-one session.[32] However, organizations may profit from a large-scale approach involving all staff rather than targeting individuals. Ultimately, conflict resolution must also address the core cause(s) of an employee's actions. "As conflict is caused by a denial of people's needs, the successful resolution must involve the satisfaction of those needs, otherwise the conflict could simmer and re-ignite. If you want a lasting win, look for the win for the other."[33]

Diversity Training

The American Library Association has made equity, diversity, and inclusion fundamental values and one of its key action areas.[34] Among the goals in the ALA's "Staff Diversity and Inclusion Action Plan" are to "increase staff training concerning diversity and inclusiveness in the workplace."[35] Diversity training can be defined as "programs aimed at facilitating positive intergroup interactions, reducing prejudice and discrimination, and enhancing the skills, knowledge, and motivation of people to interact with diverse others."[36] The ALA provides some webinars on diversity issues online at ODLOS Webinar Archives.

Diversity training can take the form of workshops, courses, mentoring sessions, or stand-alone methods. A study of 283 academic mentor/mentee pairings over an eight-hour training saw 47 percent of participants increase their diversity awareness and 16 percent report behavioral change.[37] In a 2012 study of 178 publications on diversity training, the more effective training methods were found to be results-oriented and yielded an increase in both skills and knowledge in a formal setting.[38] Research indicates that diversity training is best when "embedded and complemented by other diversity-related initiatives, [and there is] genuine organizational commitment and support."[39] Incorporating this training into other organization activities such as cultural events, coursework, and campus initiatives in the education setting results in more pronounced positive change.[40]

Other characteristics of successful training include a focus on several different kinds of diversity rather than simply one group; that is, including all kinds of diversity (race, ethnicity, religion, handicap, etc.) in the discussion so that everyone feels included.[41] Additionally, it is important for the diversity training's expectations and goals to align.[42] Lastly, training programs that use a variety of instructional methods "such as role playing, lectures, experiential exercises, discussion, and other learning methods" are viewed more positively.[43]

Conclusion

Through the use of organization-wide training, incivility and dysfunction can be reduced in libraries. While there are many forms this training can take, this chapter highlighted some methods in which bias, empathy, conflict management, and diversity training can take shape. While dysfunction can never be completely eliminated, the research presented in this chapter and throughout the book indicates that these types of trainings can make a difference. Libraries can take on the challenge through training implementation and start to make positive changes in their organization and in the library field as a whole.

QUESTIONS FOR REFLECTION

- What is the current status of the library organization's workplace?

- What training(s) are critically important to make improvements in the workplace?

- How can these trainings be addressed: in-house or externally?

- What is the library organization's long-term plan for addressing workplace incivility and maintaining a positive work environment in the future?

NOTES

1. Cheryl Staats, Kelly Capatosto, Lena Tenney, and Sarah Mamo, "State of the Science: Implicit Bias Review," Kirwan Institute, Ohio State University, 2017 Edition, p. 8, http://kirwaninstitute.osu.edu/implicit-bias-training/resources/2017-implicit-bias -review.pdf.
2. Shamika Dalton and Michele Villagran, "Minimizing and Addressing Implicit Bias in the Workplace: Be Proactive, Part One," *College & Research Library News* 79, no. 9 (2018), https://crln.acrl.org/index.php/crlnews/article/view/17370/19151.
3. Tarica LaBossiere, Endia Paige, and Beau Steenken, "Keeping Up with . . . Implicit Bias," Association of College & Research Libraries, http://www.ala.org/acrl/ publications/keeping_up_with/bias.
4. Beverly J. Glover, "The Role of HR in Managing Workplace Bias," Oklahoma City Human Resources Society, PowerPoint presentation, https://www.ochrs.org/sites/ ochrs2/uploads/images/meetings/OCHRS_HR_Role_in_Managing_Workplace _Bias.pdf.

5. Tarica LaBossiere, Endia Paige, and Beau Steenken, "What Is Implicit Bias?" Association of College & Research Libraries, http://www.ala.org/acrl/publications/keeping_up_with/bias.

6. Glover, "The Role of HR in Managing Workplace Bias."

7. India R. Johnson, Brandon M. Kopp, and Richard E. Petty, "Just Say No! (and Mean It): Meaningful Negation as a Tool to Modify Automatic Racial Attitudes," *Group Processes & Intergroup Relations*, March 25, 2016: 1–23.

8. Staats et al., "State of the Science: Implicit Bias Review," 57.

9. Magnus Englander, "Empathy Training from a Phenomenological Perspective," *Journal of Phenomenological Psychology* 45, no. 1 (2014): 10.

10. Edwin Ritsch, "Manual: Empathy Training," Center for Building a Culture of Empathy and Compassion, http://cultureofempathy.com/References/Experts/Others/Files/Marieke-Kingma-Empathy-Training-Manual.pdf.

11. Tony Chiu Ming Lam, Klodiana Kolomitro, and Flanny C. Alamparambil, "Empathy Training: Methods, Evaluation, Practices, and Validity," *Journal of MultiDisciplinary Evaluation* 7, no. 16 (July 2011): 162.

12. Katelyn Angell, "Applications of Edith's Stein's Empathy Theory to Library Science," *Library and Information Research* 35, no. 110 (2011): 24.

13. Beatrice Calvin and Jamie Bragg, eds., "Empathy: Tips for Improving Workplace Interactions," *Library Worklife* 16, no. 2 (February 11, 2019), http://ala-apa.org/newsletter/2019/02/11/empathy-tips-for-improving-workplace-interactions/.

14. Lam, Kolomitro, and Alamparambil, "Empathy Training," 162.

15. Lam, Kolomitro, and Alamparambil, "Empathy Training," 166.

16. Lam, Kolomitro, and Alamparambil, "Empathy Training," 175.

17. Lam, Kolomitro, and Alamparambil, "Empathy Training," 175.

18. Englander, "Empathy Training from a Phenomenological Perspective," 20.

19. Derald Wing Sue, *Microaggressions in Everyday Life: Race, Gender and Sexual Orientation* (Hoboken, NJ: John Wiley & Sons, 2010), 5.

20. Derald Wing Sue et al., "Racial Microaggressions in Everyday Life: Implications for Clinical Practice," *American Psychologist* 62, no. 4 (2007): 274.

21. Sue et al., "Racial Microaggressions in Everyday Life," 274.

22. Sue et al., "Racial Microaggressions in Everyday Life," 274.

23. Elvia Arroyo-Ramirez et al., "The Reach of a Long-Arm Stapler: Calling in Microaggressions in the LIS Field through Zine Work," *Library Trends* 67, no. 1 (summer 2018): 15.

24. Nicole A. Cooke, "Pushing Back from the Table: Fighting to Maintain My Voice as a Pre-Tenure Minority Female in the White Academy," *Polymath: An Interdisciplinary Arts & Sciences Journal* 4, no. 2 (2014): 39–49; Jaena Alabi, "Racial Microaggressions in Academic Libraries: Results of a Survey of Minority and Non-Minority Librarians," *Journal of Academic Librarianship* 41, no. 1 (January 2015): 47–53.

25. Sue et al., "Racial Microaggressions in Everyday Life," 274.

26. Catherine Edwards and Graham Walton, "Change and Conflict in the Academic Library," *Library Management* 21, no. 1 (2000): 41.

27. Jo Henry, Joe Eshleman, Rebecca Croxton, and Richard Moniz, "Incivility and Dysfunction in the Library Workplace: Perceptions and Feedback from the Field," *Journal of Library Administration* 58, no. 2 (2018): 140.

28. Lawrence Susskind, Sarah McKeaman, and Jennifer Thomas-Larmer, *The Consensus Building Handbook: A Comprehensive Guide to Reaching Agreement* (Thousand Oaks, CA: Sage, 1999), 104.

29. Susskind, McKeaman, and Thomas-Larmer, *Consensus Building Handbook,* 114.

30. Susskind, McKeaman, and Thomas-Larmer, *Consensus Building Handbook,* 120–21.

31. Kathryn Tyler, "Helping Employees Cool It," *HRMAgazine* 55, no. 4 (2010): 56.

32. Tyler, "Helping Employees Cool It," 56.

33. Shay McConnon and Margaret McConnon, *Conflict Management in the Workplace* (Begbroke, UK: How-to Content, 2008), 50.

34. American Library Association, "Issues & Advocacy: Equity, Diversity, and Inclusion," http://www.ala.org/advocacy/diversity.

35. American Library Association, "American Library Association Staff Diversity and Inclusion Action Plan," http://www.ala.org/aboutala/sites/ala.org.aboutala/files/content/diversity/ALA_Diversity_Action_and_Inclusion_Plan.pdf.

36. Katerina Bezrukova, Karen A. Jehn, and Chester S. Spell, "Reviewing Diversity Training: Where We Have Been and Where We Should Go," *Academy of Management Learning & Education* 11, no. 2 (2012): 208.

37. Stephanie C. House, Kimberly C. Spencer, and Christine Pfund, "Understanding How Diversity Training Impacts Faculty Mentors' Awareness and Behaviors," *International Journal of Mentoring and Coaching in Education* 7, no. 1 (2018): 75–76.

38. Bezrukova, Jehn, and Spell, "Reviewing Diversity Training," 213.

39. Bezrukova, Jehn, and Spell, "Reviewing Diversity Training," 214.

40. Bezrukova, Jehn, and Spell, "Reviewing Diversity Training," 215.

41. Bezrukova, Jehn, and Spell, "Reviewing Diversity Training," 216.

42. Bezrukova, Jehn, and Spell, "Reviewing Diversity Training," 218.

43. Bezrukova, Jehn, and Spell, "Reviewing Diversity Training," 218.

ABOUT THE AUTHORS

JO HENRY is reference and instruction librarian at the Horry-Georgetown Technical College Library (Georgetown Campus), South Carolina. Previously she was a librarian at the Charlotte Mecklenburg Library and the information services librarian at South Piedmont Community College. She obtained her MLIS from the University of North Carolina Greensboro and a master's degree in public administration from Georgia Southern University. She has coauthored four books: *Fundamentals for the Academic Liaison* (2014), *The Personal Librarian: Enhancing the Student Experience* (2014), *The Mindful Librarian* (2016), and *The Dysfunctional Library: Challenges and Solutions to Workplace Relationships* (2017). Henry has presented at numerous library conferences and has co-facilitated library workshops (alongside Richard Moniz and Joe Eshleman) both online and in North Carolina and South Carolina.

JOE ESHLEMAN is senior librarian at Central Piedmont Community College in Charlotte, North Carolina. He was previously the instruction librarian at the Johnson & Wales University Library–Charlotte from 2008 to 2015 and was head librarian for two years at the JWU Providence library. He received his MLIS degree from the University of North Carolina at Greensboro in 2007. He has completed the Association of College & Research Libraries' Immersion Program, an intensive program of training and education for instruction librarians. Eshleman is a coauthor of *Fundamentals for the Academic Liaison* (2014), *The Mindful Librarian* (2016), and *The Dysfunctional Library: Challenges and Solutions to*

Workplace Relationships (2017). He is also a coauthor of *Librarians and Instructional Designers: Innovation and Collaboration* (2016) and a contributor to *The Personal Librarian: Enhancing the Student Experience* (2014). He has presented at numerous conferences on instructional librarianship and other topics.

RICHARD MONIZ is the director of library services at the Horry-Georgetown Technical College, which has campuses in Conway, Georgetown, and Myrtle Beach, South Carolina. He previously served as the director of library services for Johnson & Wales University's North Miami campus from 1997 to 2004 and was director of library services for Johnson & Wales University's Charlotte campus from 2004 to 2018. He is also an adjunct instructor for the University of North Carolina at Greensboro's LIS program. In addition to publishing numerous articles, Moniz is the sole author of the textbook *Practical and Effective Management of Libraries* (2010) and the coauthor or coeditor of six other books: *Fundamentals for the Academic Liaison* (2014), *The Personal Librarian: Enhancing the Student Experience* (2014), *The Mindful Librarian* (2016), *Librarians and Instructional Designers: Innovation and Collaboration* (2016), *The Dysfunctional Library: Challenges and Solutions to Workplace Relationships* (2017), and *Recipes for Mindfulness in Your Library* (2019).

INDEX